100% Jackie CHAN

The Essential Companion

Introduction by
Jackie Chan
Edited by
Richard Cooper and Mike Leeder

TITAN BOOKS

791.4302
one

100% JACKIE CHAN: THE ESSENTIAL COMPANION

1 84023 491 1

Published by
Titan Books
A division of
Titan Publishing Group Ltd
144 Southwark St
London
SE1 0UP

First edition June 2002
10 9 8 7 6 5 4 3 2

Published in conjunction with
Screen Power Publishing Group, PO Box 1989, Bath BA2 2YE
Tel/Fax +44 (0) 1225 420807 Email: office@screen-power.com
www.screen-power.com

Did you enjoy this book? We love to hear from our readers. Please e-mail us at:
readerfeedback@titanemail.com or write to Reader Feedback at the above address.
To subscribe to our regular newsletter for up-to-the-minute news, great offers and competitions, email:
titan-news@titanemail.com

Titan Books' film and TV range are available from all good bookshops or direct from our mail order service. For a free catalogue or to order, phone **01536 764646** with your credit card details, or write to **Titan Books Mail Order, AASM Ltd, Unit 6, Pipewell Industrial Estate, Desborough, Northants, NN14 2SW**. Please quote reference JC/EC

A CIP catalogue record for this title is available from the British Library.

Printed and bound in Great Britain by MPG, Bodmin, Cornwall.

11/03
BT

Acknowledgements

Richard Cooper would like to thank the following people and companies for their support, assistance, hard work and friendship in the creation of this book and the ever popular magazine.

Thanks to: The JC Group, Mike Leeder, Maggie Ku, Dorothy Wong, Todd Masinelli, Gail Mihara, Brad Allan, Matthew Edwards, Paul Williams, EMG, Laurence Ronson, Albert Valentin, Jeanne Fredriksen, Kenneth Low, Daniel Wu, Benny "The Jet" Urquidez, Francoise Yip, Sammo Hung, Stanley Tong, Jeff Yang, New Line Cinema, Renee Witterstaetter, Kevin and Toby Hudson, Golden Harvest Films Ltd, Golden Way Films Ltd, Media Asia, StarEastNet Corp. and all our loyal worldwide readers!

Very Special Thanks to: Jackie Chan, Willie Chan and Solon So for their support, assistance and ever growing friendship.

About the Editor

Richard Cooper was born on 8th April 1974 in Bath, England. He watched his first Jackie Chan movie, Drunken Master, at the age of eleven and has been hooked ever since. He graduated from the City of Bath College after two years, at the age of twenty, gaining top honours in Business and Finance.

He ventured out to Hong Kong in December 1994 to approach Jackie Chan's office about starting up an official UK based Fan Club and eight months later received their full approval and support.

In late 1997 he found interests in the publishing industry and received approval from The Jackie Chan Group to publish an official bi-monthly magazine focussed entirely on Jackie Chan. To this day, the ever-growing glossy magazine is well received by readers all over the world. These days Richard still retains a strong working relationship with Jackie and his Hong Kong office.

He is still President of the UK branch of Jackie Chan's International Fan Club, both editor and publisher of Screen Power magazine and now publisher and editor of the forthcoming Jade Screen magazine - a bi-monthly glossy publication covering the entire Hong Kong Movie Industry.

He is also hard at work developing books and video documentaries in conjunction with the above two publications.

Richard Cooper can be contacted via the following email address: office@screen-power.com

Dedication

This book is dedicated to everyone who is involved or associated with Screen Power, reads Screen Power magazine on a regular basis and/or receives a complementary copy of each issue from the Screen Power Publishing Group.

About Mike Leeder

Mike Leeder was born a long time ago, in a galaxy far far away. He first became a fan of Jackie Chan after watching a double bill of Snake in the Eagle's Shadow and Drunken Master. After completing school, college and a few years of the nine-to-five, Mike packed his bags and relocated to Hong Kong to live a life of movies, movies, movies and more movies! He has written for such magazines as Screen Power, Combat, Inside Kung Fu, Femme Fatales, Karate International, Eastern Heroes, MAMA, Impact and many more.

He has also contributed to the books The Essential Guide to Hong Kong Movies, Stefan Hammond's Sex and Zen and a Bullet in the Head, and Jackie Chan the Best of Inside Kung Fu, from Unique Publications. He was Associate Producer amongst other things on the Freemantle Asiavision documentary David Carradine's Martial Arts Journey, and has worked with Ocean Films, Videocam Films, Jet Black Productions, and Action Image on various projects. He is a founder member of Just Cause with Reuben Langdon.

He is serving as Contributing Editor to both Screen Power and Jade Screen. He is also hard at work developing various book and video documentary projects with Richard Cooper.

Contents

成 龍 影 業 有 限 公 司

· JACKIE & WILLIE ·
· PRODUCTION S   LTD ·

Hello Lovely People,

You've read the magazine, now read the book!   In this, the first Screen Power book you will be able to read everything from my recent romance action comedy "Gorgeous" to my Hollywood action comedy "Rush Hour".   If you like some of older films like "Project A" and "Armour of God II: Operation Condor" then you have come to the right place.

I produced and directed two video documentaries a couple of years ago with Media Asia, namely, "My Story" and "My Stunts" – you can read all about them here too.   And, of course, like in the magazine, there will be plenty of photos throughout.

Also don't forget that there are a number of interviews with my friends, co-stars and colleagues in this book too.   If you like this book (and I hope you do) then I am sure Richard will appreciate hearing from you all.

In the meantime, as usual, it's back to work for me!   As to what I am doing right now – no doubt you'll all be able to read about it in the magazine soon enough.

Thank you all for your continued support.

Happy reading!

JACKIE CHAN

Jackie Chan - A Profile

Western Name:	*Jackie Chan*
Chinese Name(s):	*Sing Lung, Chan Lung, Chan Kwong-sang*
Nationality:	*Chinese*
Date of Birth:	*7th April 1954*
Place of Birth:	*Hong Kong*
Main Residence:	*Hong Kong*
Height:	*5ft 8ins*
Hair:	*Black*
Eyes:	*Hazel*
Weight:	*155lbs*
Occupation(s):	*Actor, Director, Producer, Martial Arts Choreographer, Stuntman and Singer*
Passion(s):	*His Work, Cars, Fans, Friends and Family*

The Official Statistics

CATEGORY	Cms/Ins/Other
Height	173 cms/5 feet 8 inches
Shoulder Width	47/18.5
Head Circumference	60/23.5
Neck	42/16.5
Chest	105/41.5
Waist	82/32
Hip	99/39
Trouser Length	106/42
Inseam	73/29
Arm Length	60/23.5
Armpit/Shoulder	55/21.5
Shoe Size (General)	Size 8
Shoe Size (Leather)	Size 8.5

(Source: The Jackie Chan Group)

MR. NICE GUY

Review by Mike Leeder

Starring *JACKIE CHAN, MIKKI LI, GABRIELLE FITZPATRICK, KAREN MCLYMONT, RICHARD NORTON*
Cameos by *SAMMO HUNG, JOYCE GODENZI, EMIL CHAU*

Action Sequences by *JACKIE CHAN, SAMMO HUNG, CHO WING, JACKIE CHAN STUNTMEN'S CLUB*

Directed by *SAMMO HUNG*

Screen Power's 'Hong Kong Correspondent' Mike Leeder reviews Jackie's latest rumble filmed down under!

It's Jackie Chan to the rescue again, and again in his latest - 'Mr. Nice Guy' (Chinese name: 'Yat Gor Ho Yan'). In his latest film, directed by Sammo Hung, Jackie plays Jackie(!!!), world renowned chef and host of the top rated TV show 'What's Cooking Tonight'.

The story really starts when a video tape of Jackie's latest show gets accidentally swapped with a news-reporter's video tape of a gangland slaying. Of course, the two rival gangs want to get their hands on the tape at any cost, which leaves Jackie having to do just what he does best - getting the better of the bad guys! Which he achieves by leaping between buildings, dodging bullets and performing some truly incredible martial arts.

I will be honest when I say that I didn't really like Jackie's previous movie 'First Strike/Police Story 4'. I thought the film dragged but it went on to be the biggest movie of last year's Asian box-office.

But 'Mr. Nice Guy' is the best film Jackie's done since 'Rumble in the Bronx'. This film starts off at high speed and doesn't let up. The long awaited reunion of Jackie and Sammo - this time remaining behind the camera apart from a hilarious cameo - provides the goods in abundance.

Hell's Angel wedding

Highlights of the movie for me include Jackie's demonstration of culinary kung fu expertise during the opening credits.
Jackie's first fight

Jackie battles it out with Australian actor Richard Norton in 'Mr. Nice Guy'

and on-going fight chase through alleyways and a Hell's Angel wedding. A bone-crunching fight and chase through a shopping mall on a horse and buggy with Jackie continuing to fight his pursuers as the buggy rides down a crowded street. A great close quarters fight scene in a van full of villains that provides Sammo with his hilarious cameo - clad all in skin tight cycling gear! There's a great building site fight with Jackie flipping and kicking to the max and making great use of various props. And much, much more.

Thunderbirds puppet!

The fight between Richard Norton (playing druglord Giancarlo) and Jackie is also great fun - with Jackie unable to let loose to full effect due to being strung up like a Thunderbirds puppet! (See the photos from the first issue of Screen Power on this fight scene.) And as for the finale, well... I think you'd better go see the movie... !!!!!

The supporting cast is good. Taiwanese actress Mikki Lee makes a very attractive leading lady, while Australian actresses Fitzpatrick and McLymont try their best. Richard Norton doesn't do much in the way of fighting, he's artfully doubled by stuntmaster Cho Wing for one jumping kick but he is suitably villainous.

somewhat reminiscent

The aforementioned cameo by Sammo Hung is hilarious, and his wife Joyce Godenzi appears just to grab a bite to eat. While singer Emil Chau's cameo is somewhat reminiscent of his cameo in another Jackie movie and works even better because of its familiarity.

Former Hong Kong based gwailo boys Jonathan Isadore, last seen on screen with Jackie as an Arab in 'Operation Condor: Armour of God II', and my old flat-mate Habby Heske from Van Damme's 'The Quest' make the most of their screen time, and the Australian stuntmen certainly make a better job of the Hong Kong choreography than a lot of guys. The action is choreographed by Jackie, his stunt team, Sammo with the aid of his son Timmy Hung, and former Tsui Siu Ming student and bootman extraordinaire Cho Wing of 'Bury Me High' and 'Nocturnal Demon' fame.

All in all a most enjoyable film and one that is certain to do the business at the box-office internationally just as it already has in Asia. My only quibbles were that while it was shot in English, Hong Kong audiences got a Cantonese-dubbed print which most Hong Kong people complained about, saying it was stupid to have everyone speaking Chinese, and lastly that the end credit outtakes show a whole section of mouthwatering combat not seen in the finished print!

Yammo Gow Chor....!!!

Factoids:

Mr. Nice Guy was the film that first introduced Jackie to Brad Allan, Paul Andreovski and Siros Niaros.

Gabrielle Fitzpatrick later went on to star with Van Damme in Inferno/Desert Heat.

Mr. Nice Guy was to have been called Superchef for the US market, until sound minds prevailed.

Jackie tied-up behind-the-scenes of 'Mr. Nice Guy'

ROTTERDAM
(Or Anywhere!)

Screen Power editor Richard Cooper goes on set and takes a look behind the scenes at Jackie Chan's latest (and possibly greatest) action movie, shooting in and around Rotterdam - 'Who Am I?'

The sun rises over the oddly shaped buildings and endless canals that make up the streets of Rotterdam. It's going to be another sunny day - perfect conditions for filming.

Jackie has made movies in many parts of the world including locations as diverse as Yugoslavia, the Ukraine and the Sahara Desert but this time it's Rotterdam, Holland. The reason for filming here is quite simply because Jackie fell in love with the architecture and the extreme European culture when he was invited to the Rotterdam Film Festival on 30th January 1997. Now in the middle of August (and after three months of shooting in South Africa) he's back with some members of the Jackie Chan Stuntmen's Club and the entire cast and crew to film the next segment of 'Who Am I?'

Upon initial observations a Jackie Chan movie set is just how you would expect it to be - manic, noisy and very atmospheric! The cast are busy reciting their lines with tremendous South African accents, Jackie's stunt team practise their acrobatics and martial arts and the film crew try to unravel what looks like miles of twisted cables. In the middle of all this confusion sits Jackie, busy psyching himself up for a big fight scene - busy psyching himself up? Of course! The entire world will look at this next scene (which although it will take about a week to shoot, will actually last around four or five minutes on screen) therefore it has to be great, something very new and something that will please his millions of fans all over the world... yeah, quite a responsibility for one man - but hey! Hang on a minute this is Jackie Chan!

I like filming in Rotterdam.

Upon seeing me he leaps out of his chair, smiles, punches me in the arm, shakes my hand warmly and offers me a glass of Coca-Cola! Literally in that order! After a quick drink I ask him the first thing that comes into my head ("This is the first time you have filmed in Europe since "Operation Condor". How do you find filming here?") - and from the look on his face I could easily tell he'd been asked that question a few hundred times that week already! "I like filming in Rotterdam. The heat is not so bad as the Sahara Desert or the weather in South Africa! So this way makes it easier for me and the crew to film action - this movie will have big action, my trademark - you'll see!"

Benny Chan is the director this time around - a man responsible for other Hong Kong action pictures including "The Big Bullet" and "A Moment Of Romance" - although it is quite apparent that Jackie is still very much in charge of the whole production and Benny still reports directly to him on every aspect of the film.

A number of the crew behind the camera are of Australian origin and have seemingly continued to follow Jackie's globetrotting around the world after shooting "First Strike" and "Mr. Nice Guy" back in the land down under and also the first part of "Who Am I?" in South Africa. And, lastly, members of an Australian based action/stunt team who scuffled with Jackie in "Mr. Nice Guy" are back for more punishment in this film too!

Jackie and his stunt team plan out the roof-top fight scene in downtown Rotterdam

Jackie arrives on the set at about eight-thirty in the morning and shooting begins a little after that. The first thing I notice about Jackie is how much fitter he looks and acts than he did at our previous meeting eleven months earlier in London.

In fact he looks as though he wants to take on the whole world, and the way his career is going at the moment who can blame him. Rumours were going around that Jackie had been training extra hard for this movie - and to be honest I don't think they can be rumours at all, because he literally looks incredible!

"I have a big stunt to do"

Apart from an hour or so for lunch, shooting finishes around seven in the evening. From here Jackie will drive himself, his personal assistant Osumi and longtime script writer Edward Tang back to the hotel where he'll have a bite to eat and then start his rigorous daily three hour training session in the hotel gym. "You know what? I don't need to sleep much - I just save it all for when I go on promotion tours when I have to travel so much and there is nothing really to do but sleep - I only really sleep a lot when I have a big stunt to do" Jackie said.

As all the people involved in the production arrive the right amount of drama and continuity. All of it leads to an exhausting time for everyone involved and at the end of some days it seems like a wasted effort for all the work that went into just a few seconds of finished material. That is why good humour and patience are abundant on the set. It must be very satisfying for Jackie when a film is completed. To sit back and see it on the big screen is when you realise all the sweat, pain and very hard work was worthwhile...

There are times on the set when some of the cast and crew are not needed for a particular shot, which for them means spending most of the day sitting around doing nothing. Many of them use this opportunity to learn their lines, train or just fool around to pass the time. On one occasion, some of Jackie's stunt team put out several mats to practise acrobatics on. Of course, they each try and outdo each other by performing more and more demanding flips - until someone is hurt! But still, like Jackie, they just laugh it off. Pain does not seem to be a problem for them either...

One of the cast is the very laid back Ron Smerczak, who is originally from Blackpool in the UK but now resides in South Africa. He counts himself very

"To sit back and see it on the big screen is when you realise all the sweat, pain and very hard work was worthwhile..."

at the set early in the morning, they all help themselves to cups of extra-strong coffee. After all, they are going to need it for the hard day's work that lies ahead of them. Jackie does not touch the coffee and instead drinks a strange green icy substance - which is apparently made from peas. In this instance Jackie was a bit annoyed with the drink and could not quench his thirst because it was too frozen!

an exhausting time

During filming Jackie is always very focussed on the set. Even if a take seems to go perfectly, he will nearly always have another attempt just to see if he can make it better. For example, a simple dialogue scene will be re-shot again and again just to gain

lucky to get a co-starring role alongside Jackie. "I'm so pleased I went along to the audition now" (laughing), says Ron. The excitement for Ron lies in the fact that this film will show in cinemas all over the world. Ron also commented, "Who knows, it might bring in more projects for me in the future. I mean you can't go wrong having a co-starring role in the latest Jackie Chan movie. I have found this kind of filming rather exciting so I do hope to work with Jackie again in the future."

A one-on rap session with the man himself on set:

Jackie Chan:

You know what? I just hurt my old injury again - my neck, from "Mr. Nice Guy".

Richard Cooper:

Oh no, what happened? Are you okay?

JC: Don't worry I'm okay. After filming today I go to the hotel gym and train with weights (Jackie demonstrates lifting weights) - but I push too many weights on my back and Bop! - gone again!

RC: Does that mean the shooting will stop tomorrow?

JC: No, still shooting.

RC: In your films - you always seem to show something very new each time. In "First Strike" you use a snowboard and in "Rumble in the Bronx" you learn to water-ski barefoot. When I watched you in town today, you were riding a Dutch bicycle (the wheels are where the handlebars should be!) in a chase sequence - you fell off a few times, but after about ten minutes you were okay and got the shot.

JC: Of course. I always like to show something new on the big screen. I don't care about really learning these things, I just do it - even if I really want to learn these things I can't anyway because I have no time (laughing).

RC: Just for the movie?

JC: Yeah, for my movie - then go somewhere else and try something new. I like new, many people say, "Oh, Jackie you do so many things in your movies but soon you will get no more ideas." No, it's not true, because I still have so many ideas based on twenty years experience.

RC: You have a lot of notes written down in your book for future ideas?

JC: Yes, I quickly write it down - ah, you know these things!

RC: I have been talking to Edward your scriptwriter. He says he has been writing most of your films since you joined Golden Harvest back in 1980, starting off with "The Young Master". How much input or say does Edward have in your films?

JC: Oh, I know a story about Edward Tang (laughing).

RC: What happened?

JC: In the very beginning he was very quiet! I was an uprising star, getting known all over Asia in my mid-twenties. He wrote the scripts out for me. I wrote things in brackets - I say "Why do you put this?" He says, "I don't know!" So I tell him, "I don't like it, change it!" Nowadays (laughing), if I say, "I don't like this, change it!" Edward will say, "Jackie, you don't like it? Why not?" Now it's all very different. Edward understands me a lot, like also my stunt guys

Jackie with 'Who Am I?' Director Benny Chan and actor Ron Smerczak in the basement location

- all my big family. You know what? Some of them have been with me for like twenty years now.

RC: *Like Willie? [Willie Chan, Manager/Agent/ Business Partner]*

JC: Yes, like Willie.

RC: *Before I came over to Rotterdam, I read in some other magazines that you were training even harder nowadays. Is that true? And also you said that you were fitter now than you were ten years ago.*

JC: You know what? I think more smarter now (Jackie smiles) - you know, more experience. Of course I still train every day. Very hard - but I always have trained, every day back then.

RC: *Was it true you said, "There are new young actors who can punch and kick faster than me, but if you give me a month to film any punch, kick or flip - I'll make it look faster than anyone!"*

JC: Do you think I say that?

RC: *Yes! (laughing)*

JC: Ah, you're right! And it's true! (laughing)

RC: *After "Who Am I?" will you be making "Rush Hour"?*

JC: Nothing signed yet! The thing with America is everything is talking, too much talking - just talk one year and do nothing.

RC: *If you make "Rush Hour" will you direct it?*

JC: No - only direct the fights and stunts. Also with "Rush Hour" they have a contract that I have to sign that I will not cut the movie until after three months - yes, it's true!

RC: *So, after three months you can make it more to your style and taste?*

JC: Yes, true Jackie Chan style!

RC: *If you don't make "Rush Hour" next what other film do you think you'll be doing? You don't have to tell me if you don't want to.*

JC: No, I think maybe "Police Story - Part 5" and shoot it in Istanbul - it looks good there.

RC: *A Jackie Chan movie shooting in Turkey - that sounds good and will definitely please your Western fans.*

JC: Really? You think so?

RC: *Yes, or you could make a film in England.*

Jackie watches the world go by as the crew set up the next shot in downtown Rotterdam, Holland

"Police Story 5" in England sounds good too.

JC: Actually I want to film in London for a movie one day. You will of course know when, okay - but right now is Rotterdam and before South Africa. The thing is, London is very expensive to shoot a movie, just like America and Japan - that's why I film in Australia, Canada, South Africa and now in Rotterdam because it's much cheaper but still good for my movie. We are not filming in these places because it is too expensive - if the script really says, "Oh, Jackie you have to film in London or wherever" then I have to come, but with my movies we are concerned more with spending money on the action and stunts than just to film in some place.

I left the "Who Am I?" set with a greater knowledge of how much work goes into a movie. In the end, a major factor in helping a film come together is teamwork - abundant in a Jackie Chan production.

Any last words from Jackie?

With me it's like - I always want to make movies my way! Every Chinese New Year, everyone wants to see a Jackie Chan movie. So this way I cannot disappoint them. But, I will make more Hollywood movies - but Jackie Chan Hollywood movies - you'll see!

Jackie in Malaysia filming the opening scenes to 'Who Am I?'

by Mike Leeder

WHO AM I?

R e v i e w

Starring/Action Choreographed By/Directed By: Jackie Chan
Also Starring: Michelle Ferre, Mimi Yamamoto, Ron Smerczak
Directed By: Benny Chan
English Language. Running time: 2 hours
Golden Harvest Pictures Ltd. 1998

Jackie Chan is back on the screen in a very big way. On the small screen there is the recent release of Media Asia's/JC Group's most impressive 'Jackie Chan: My Story' documentary. This is now to be followed by 'Jackie Chan: My Stunts' set to go before the cameras at the end of January, and a TV series based on Jackie's 'Police Story' movies, both new projects being developed by Media Asia. Jackie completed filming on 'Who Am I?' in early November and immediately flew to Hollywood to commence filming of 'Rush Hour', he flew back for his Fan Club party and the Jackie Chan Exhibition in Hong Kong (If you were there, glad to have seen you, if not, where were you?) and his

eagerly awaited film 'Who Am I?' hit cinemas yesterday. I was there and bring you the first (I think!) review, exclusively for SCREEN POWER.

The film opens with Jackie as a member of a multi-national commando team working for the CIA. Their mission, to kidnap a group of scientists from the African jungle, and to retrieve a formula for an incredibly powerful new power source. The mission is accomplished but Jackie and his team are doublecrossed by CIA operative Morgan. The rest of the team is killed but Jackie survives albeit suffering from numerous injuries and total amnesia. Luckily he is found by a native tribe that nurses him back to health, and who give Jackie the name "Who am I?" because he asks this question so much. Jackie recovers his health and becomes a member of the tribe, but when one of the tribe discovers wreckage containing possible clues to Jackie's identity, Jackie realizes that he can't rest until he knows his true identity.

When Jackie crosses paths with stranded rally driver Yuki (Mimi Yamamoto) and her injured brother, he is able to rescue them and catch a ride back to civilization. Yuki takes Jackie to an amnesia specialist for help, only for the bad guys to see Jackie's face in the paper and send assassins to kill him. Jackie also attracts the attention of Christine (Michelle Ferre), a reporter (or is she?) who sees Jackie as the story of a lifetime. As Jackie struggles to piece together his disjointed memories, he, Yuki and Christine find themselves having to team up and battle Morgan's hitmen. A vital clue reveals that the key to Jackie's identity waits in Rotterdam.

Jackie and Christine fly to the Netherlands, but find themselves being chased throughout Rotterdam by Morgan's men. The villains know that if Jackie lives he will ruin their plans and order him to be killed on sight. Jackie must face the combined forces of corrupt CIA operatives and local thugs in a fight to the finish if he is to ever find out just "Who Am I?" (Well, "Who He Is" actually but it doesn't sound as good does it!)

The Big Question: Did I Like It? Yes, it's a very enjoyable fast paced English language action adventure that should not only do very well at the box office but also please most fans of Jackie's work. Jackie handles the English dialogue and the action with aplomb. Anyone who has had any doubts about his physical abilities of late will be blown away by Jackie as he flips, kicks, punches and takes hits without equal. It's not the best Jackie Chan film ever made, but it's still a very good one and worth more than a bit of your time and attention.

Japanese actresses Mimi Yamamoto and Michelle Ferre turn in more than adequate performances as Jackie's two female leads, with Ms. Yamamoto coming out slightly ahead in the performance stakes. Ron Smerczak is suitably slimey as the treacherous Morgan, while veteran actor Ed Nelson uses his years of experience to play the corrupt CIA chief,

The General. Amongst the supporting cast, actor/ stuntman Kwan Yeung gets to strut his stuff nicely as he and the very flexible Dutch bootman Ron Smoorenburg take on Jackie in the finale. It's not only a good fight, it nicely mixes the excitement with some comedy to spice it up and it's a lengthy fight too. Fans of Sho Kosugi should keep an eye out for a brief appearance by the former shinobi star's son Kane Kosugi as a Japanese commando in the opening alongside former Jackie Chan bodyguard Ken Low as a non-kicking Korean commando. Michael "Learns To Rock" Lambert crops up several times throughout the film in a non-fighting role as a scar faced henchman with the appearance of a 60s Beatnik poet, while occasional Gwailo boys Steve Baretta, David Slumbers and TJ the Swede turn up as commandos in the opening, and my old partner in crime Russ "The Singing Welsh Cyborg" Price appears in a non-fighting role as a suavely dressed bodyguard in Rotterdam.

Several set pieces stand out: Jackie's first real burst of martial artistry as he takes on a team of shadowy

Jackie - the South African Warrior!

assassins in a deserted arena and makes an incredible escape, the fight in a Sun City hotel complex complete with some incredible physical stunts, several very well shot car chases, a lengthy and spectacular fight and chase through Rotterdam including a clog fight(!) and the heart pumping finale as Jackie battles his way through numerous minor league goons before taking on Ah Yeung and the kicking Dutchman in a fight to the finish. Jackie's back to full physical fitness despite what anyone else may claim, he's busting moves all over the shop in this film, his kicks and punches are as sharp as ever. Kudos to Jackie and his stunt-team - Sam Wong, Man Ching, Gunn, Andy Cheng, and his new Australian stunt-boys for doing a hell of a job with the action. It's crisply choreographed and my only complaint is that there isn't enough of it! There is plenty of action, car stunts, high falls, explosions, gunplay, and the several fight scenes are superb but you just want more! (Well I do, there's no pleasing me sometimes!)

The finished film flows incredibly well with Jackie making good use of the James Bond styled storyline, and is far more exciting and enjoyable than 'First Strike', which also attempted to be a 007 styled actioner. What is disappointing is that obviously a lot of footage was deleted from the final print. The section in Africa involving Jackie and the tribe was far longer and featured several scenes I was looking forward to seeing, including Jackie's rhino ride and battle with poachers, but they didn't make the final print. But I do remember that before Jackie and his crew went to Malaysia to film the opening, the word was that they had already assembled two and a half hours of finished footage and were even considering releasing the film in two parts, and who knows maybe some of the missing footage will be re-instated for the international release of the film. The film was originally announced to be directed by Benny Chan who had previously helmed such diverse films as 'A Moment Of Romance' with Andy Lau, 'The Magic Crane' with Anita Mui and Hong Kong cinema's best film of 1996 'The Big Bullet' starring Lau Ching-wan, and while the film does feature certain elements of his directorial style, the film is very much Jackie Chan's film and deservedly warrants the "directed by Jackie Chan" credit that comes up at the beginning. Throw in some great out-takes for the end credits, a good soundtrack and a very sing-alongable (is it a word?) theme song sung by Emil Chau, great action set-pieces both physical and vehicle wise, a real James Bond-ish storyline, and the inimitable Jackie Chan and Golden Harvest have, deservedly so, another hit on their hands.

Factoids:

Michelle Ferre underwent martial arts training from J.C. stunt-teamers Andy Cheng and Sam Wong for the film as can be seen in the Making of Who Am I?, but her jump spin kick during the finale is performed by none other than a bewigged Brad Allan.

Ron Smoorenburg was recently reunited with Who Am I? director Benny Chan and action director Nicky Li for the Media Asia produced Gen-Y Cops, where he performs an opening fight scene and minor stuntwork.

While Brad Allan performed doubling in the movie, Jackie's other Australian stuntman Paul Andreovski turns up as the lime green suited hoodlum in the clog scene.

Certain elements of the Who Am I? storyline were borrowed for other movies. The amnesiac plot had been developed by Jackie years earlier, but had been lifted for Once Upon A Time in China and America, and the darker original storyline for Who Am I? ended up forming the basis of Media Asia's Purple Storm.

FRANCOISE YIP

"The Girl Who Put The Rumble In The Bronx."

By Mike Leeder

Canadian actress Francoise Yip (Yip Fong-wah) smouldered onto the big screen making her debut in Jackie Chan's 'Rumble in the Bronx'. Since the film's worldwide record breaking success, she's launched a very successful career in Hong Kong cinema. Mike Leeder caught up with the ever lovely Ms. Yip in Hong Kong to interview her for 'Screen Power'.

Filmography

* RUMBLE IN THE BRONX
* INFATUATION
* WILD
* HOW TO MEET THE LUCKY STARS
* MR. MUMBLES
* ON FIRE
* WEB OF DECEPTION
* FUTURE SPORT
* ROMEO MUST DIE

Main Picture: Francoise takes up aim in 'Mr. Mumbles'

Francoise and JC in 'Rumble'

Screen Power:

Francoise, can I start off by asking you for some basic biographical details. Where were you born and raised?

Francoise Yip:

I was born and raised in Vancouver, British Columbia. I'm a fifth generation Canadian Chinese on my father's side.

SP: *How did you first get involved in modeling and acting?*

FY: I didn't really have any lifelong ambition to be a model, until a friend of mine back home in Canada who was a successful model told me that she was getting to do a lot of travelling as a model, and this sounded pretty cool, so I thought I'd give it a try! (Laughing) I know that sounds pretty shallow that I only really got into modeling because of the prospects of travelling, but that's pretty much what got me started. (Short pause) I started off doing print ads, and got into doing television because so many shows are filmed in Vancouver. Not that I really did much in any of the shows, I was a background artist, (laughing) hired to look pretty and not say anything.

SP: *How did you get the role of Nancy in "Rumble in the Bronx"?*

FY: Quite easily! (Laughing) It was about the second or third audition I'd ever gone to and I got the role pretty much straight away. The film's director Stanley Tong and a lot of the production crew had been in Vancouver for some time doing preproduction and local casting. They had seen a lot of people for the role of Nancy but hadn't really liked anyone they saw. I auditioned on the Friday, and was filming on the Tuesday. (Laughing) I think I pretty much fit their idea of how Nancy should look and that was it. I was thrown in at the deep-end as far as acting goes; I'd never had a speaking part before and here I was as the third lead in such a big project. (Laughing) I think I learnt more in the 5 months we filmed than I could ever learn in 5 years at acting school!

SP: *Was it an easy shoot?*

FY: It was very hard for me at first, I was very nervous at playing such a big role in my first film and I had to learn to memorize lots of dialogue and directions very quickly, it made me learn what to do very quickly. I think what helped me was the fact that I lived in Vancouver, I could have a bad day and go home and spend it with my family and friends which helped me get by, while the majority of the cast and crew were stuck thousands of miles from their friends and family. I started to enjoy the shoot after about the second or third day.

SP: *For a first movie, you acquit yourself well.*

FY: (Laughing) It's awful, but that's okay because it's my first film. Is that what you're trying to say? (Laughing) I think I did okay, I could have been a lot worse but I also could have done better.

SP: *What was it like working with Jackie Chan?*

FY: It was a great experience. Before this film I think I'd only ever seen Jackie in a couple of movies, 'Cannonball Run 2' where he just had cameos and in 'Drunken Master 2', he's incredible in that! Meeting him for the first time was pretty nerve racking, we had been filming for a couple of days before he arrived in Canada and the first night he came on set there was a change in the atmosphere on set. Everybody seemed energized and were working harder than before, they all seemed more focused. It was obvious that he was the boss and the crew respected him and wanted to do their best work for him. I was introduced to him and while he seemed at first somewhat unapproachable, he very quickly revealed his true self, very easy going, and easy to get along with. He has a special way of making you feel comfortable and at ease. If you make a mistake, he makes you feel that it's okay. He's not at all snobby or stand offish.

Francoise, JC, director Stanley Tong and crew of 'Rumble in the Bronx'

SP: *One of your most memorable scenes in the movie sees you dancing pink bikini clad in a cage with a tiger! How did you feel about this scene?*

FY: It was interesting! (Laughing) To say the least! For this scene, they had two different tigers and just one actress! The problem was that after about twenty minutes the tigers would get bored and lose interest in me, and with all the heat from the lights on set, they would slink off to the corner of the cage and go to sleep! To keep the tigers looking ferocious and actively growling, they would alternate between the two tigers to get the shots they needed. Then somebody had the great idea that hanging a chunk of raw meat above me, out of sight of the cameras, would get their attention. So I was stuck in this inner cage with the tigers in the outer cage and a piece of meat hanging over me, that would not only drip blood on me every so often but also rapidly began to stink! (Laughing) The glamour of movie making. I was dancing in that cage for about 3 days, for about 12 to 14 hours straight. The tigers would get alternated and lots of attention, but I was stuck in the cage all the time.

SP: *In the original Hong Kong print of the film, you use your voice apart from a brief overdub when someone else voices you speaking Cantonese. But for New Line's international release, everybody but Jackie was redubbed including yourself. How did you feel about this?*

FY: I understand from New Line's point of view that while the movie had been shot in sync sound, there was a large amount of dialogue in Chinese and the sync wasn't that great. And for an international release, they had to redo the sound and music and it would be too much trouble to get everybody back to reloop their lines. But (laughing) it was very weird to hear somebody else's voice speaking English every time I speak in the international print. I'm used to being redubbed for Hong Kong films when I'm dubbed into Cantonese or Mandarin. But to be redubbed into English with someone else's voice is a bit strange.

SP: *When you were making the film, did you have any idea that it would launch your career in such a big way?*

Francoise hangs around in 'Mr. Mumbles'

FY: Not at all, I really enjoyed making the film. I loved working with both Jackie and Stanley Tong but I never really thought it would help start my career in films in such a big way. I knew Jackie's films did really well in Asia and had a pretty big cult following in the West, but I don't think anybody, Jackie, Golden Harvest, or especially myself, realized just how well 'Rumble' was going to do internationally. I was ready to just go back to modeling and bit parts here and there, staying in Vancouver. I just thought that at least I'd have a decent amount of footage to show people after the film came out. But the film opened to record breaking business in Hong Kong and all of Asia, which in turn led to me getting so many offers of work in the film industry here. I'd like to thank Jackie for being so nice, so considerate, and so patient when we were filming 'Rumble' and to thank him for getting my career off to such a good start. If the chance to work with Jackie again came up, I'd be very interested.

UPDATE:

The divine Ms. Yip has since returned to Canada, where she has appeared in several television series including Earth: Final Conflict, the Wesley Snipes produced Future Sport, and was reunited with Jet Li in the Warner Brothers release Romeo Must Die. She is currently training in martial arts under Canadian Wushu maestro and Operation Condor stuntman Bruce Fontaine.

A Chat With 'The Jet'

Interviewed By Mike Leeder

Former world kick-boxing champion Benny 'The Jet' Urquidez made his name and reputation in the real world of martial arts long before he stepped into the cinematic ring. Two of his best cinematic fight scenes have been opposite Jackie Chan in the movies 'Wheels On Meals/Spartan X' and 'Dragons Forever/Cyclone Z'. I was lucky enough to spend some time with Benny while he was here in Hong Kong finishing work on Shannon Lee's action movie debut, 'Enter The Phoenix/Bang, And Now You're Dead'. Benny is somebody I have admired and respected for years long before meeting him, and since spending time with him my admiration and respect has increased greatly. He is probably, and deservedly so, one of the most widely respected martial artists in the world. Despite the urge to ask him if he had electric boots and a mohair suit (blame Elton John), I did get him to discuss his cinematic career, especially his work with Jackie Chan.

JC vs The Jet in 'Wheels on Meals'

On-guard!
JC and Yuen Biao

Screen Power:

Benny, how did the opportunity to work with Jackie Chan come about?

Benny Urquidez:

Jackie and Samo Hung had heard of me, they'd seen footage of me fighting for real in the ring and also real fighting in the movie 'Force Five'. I think they looked at what I did and thought that I was probably the closest they had seen to a Westerner doing Hong Kong style action. In 'Force Five' I'm leaping about doing kicks and flips, acrobatic reactions, and I think they liked it.

I got a phone call from someone at Golden Harvest inviting me to play the main fighting villain in 'Wheels On Meals' with Jackie Chan. I was like, "Jackie who?" (laughing) At that time, I didn't have any idea who Jackie was so I asked them if they would send me a script to look at. They said they didn't have one but they wanted me to fly out to start working as soon as possible. I thought, why not, and asked them how long they would want me for and they said two months. I told my manager Stewart, "I'm going to go and work on a Hong Kong movie with Jackie Chan," and he didn't know who he was either! But Stewart went and found out who he was. He called me back and told me that Jackie was the biggest star in Asian action cinema, like Bruce Lee only bigger. I thought that sounded interesting and I was going to have some fun. I was quite surprised when my ticket arrived, as they didn't want me to fly to Hong Kong straight away, they wanted me to go to Barcelona first.

SP: *What was it like meeting Jackie for the first time?*

BU: He sized me up! Jackie, Samo and Yuen Biao were all waiting for me when I arrived and started looking me over. They asked me if I was a fighter, and I said yeah. Then their translator started telling me about my role in the film and the kind of action they would want me to do. Jackie asked me if I could do what they wanted, and I told him that if somebody showed me what they wanted, I'd give it my best shot. Samo then asked a stuntman to run through a couple series of moves, and I copied them. Jackie and Samo looked at me, then looked at each other and then looked back at

UK Video sleeve artwork for 'Wheels on Meals' by the respectful Hong Kong Classics label

me and asked if I could do any gymnastics. I answered by doing a backflip, Jackie and Samo started smiling and asking me to do more and more stuff, which I did. Then Yuen Biao comes over, and does a few acrobatic moves and kicks and asks me to copy him. I did the same moves, and they seemed very happy. Samo then got one of the stuntmen to bring in a bag and asked me to kick it while the stuntman braced it. I asked them if they wanted me to hit hard, they nodded and I went WHAM! The bag went back and smacked the stunt guy in the face. Jackie and Samo shouted, "Very powerful," and asked me to do one of my trademark moves, a spinning back kick. They also got another bigger stunt guy to hold the bag, and I asked them just how they wanted the kick, "A little bit big or real big?" Jackie shouted "Real big!" and the first stunt guy goes and stands behind the second one and braces him as well as the bag. I threw the kick and just grazed the bag, almost hitting the first stunt guy and then wound up for a second one, BAM! Now spinning back kick is one of my favourite moves, I have a lot of power in that kick. And I think it impressed them, they had been testing me to see if I was real and what I could do, because after this they pulled me in close, and we started working off each other. They'd show me combinations, I'd copy them and then Jackie asked me if I wanted to add anything, if I had any ideas. I gave them some input and showed them a few moves, and instead of them telling me what to do, we started exchanging ideas. And Jackie and myself especially started playing off each other. When we started filming, we were only doing exteriors in Spain and a few interior shots. One of which was the scene where I go out of the castle window. They had a stuntman dressed up like me, but I told them I do my own stunts. They put a few pads on me, put a wire on me to stop me from falling and then I did the stunt. Once Jackie and co saw I was prepared and able to take a few hits, they started giving me more to do. We finished filming in Spain and then flew to Hong Kong to finish the film.

SP: *When you arrived in Hong Kong, the rumours of yourself and Jackie having a real fight, an exhibition bout, started flying.*

BU: Yeah, we flew into Hong Kong and the press of course was waiting for Jackie, Samo and Yuen Biao. They started to ask them various questions about the filming, and somebody asked Jackie what it was like to fight a world champion in the movie. And Jackie looked at me, and announced to the assembled press that he was going to fight me for real once the film was completed. I knew Jackie was joking but the press didn't and they went wild. I went along with it and said "Jackie, you know I'm a professional fighter!" Jackie nodded and said, "Yes, we will have an exhibition bout!" I told him, "In the ring I have no control, I won't take any responsibility for hurting you!" Jackie answered, "No problem!" Now, Jackie and myself had really clicked during filming and were playing off each other but everybody else seemed to think it was for real. It eventually got to the point where even I thought that it might be going to happen, because Jackie wouldn't let up. He was telling everybody that he was going to fight me. I asked him "Jackie, are we really going to put on the gloves?" and he said, "Soon, soon, soon!" I started thinking that maybe he was really going to fight me, and then Samo came in on it and he started

laying bets and making odds on who was going to win! He just made it worse because everybody knows how serious Samo is about gambling.

Towards the end of filming, I asked Jackie if we were really going to fight, and Jackie smiled and said "Never mind." I looked at him and we both knew we weren't going to fight but Jackie knew that I was for real. It's funny because later on when we were filming, there was a scene where I'm supposed to shoot a right cross then a left jab, and he's supposed to bob left and weave around it. When we were filming, Jackie forgot the combination. Samo called "Action," we did the first exchange and Jackie drew a blank, I was already throwing the left. But luckily, I just managed to stop it on the very edge of his face. Jackie looked at me, his eyes were all wide and he said, "Thank you!" He had drawn a blank and frozen. Now I had bare knuckles and was going in with good power. I was throwing my whole body weight towards him, and if I'd connected I would have broken his nose or cheekbone. Jackie had been telling me to use more power, he wanted to show the power of the movement in the fight. From that point on Jackie and me got really close, he knew I was the real deal and that we were both the same - professionals. After that Jackie was always really close to me, he would always be putting his arm around me and would hug me. Now I'm a very emotional and physical person, but I wasn't used to someone who wasn't family doing that to me. Then I realised that was how Jackie looked at me, our rapport was very much like brothers and that's why he treated me like that.

SP: *Looking back at the finished film, what do you think of it?*

BU: I thought to myself that I'd had so much fun making the film, that I couldn't really believe that I had gotten paid to do it. Looking back at it, yes I got some bruises, bumps and lumps when we were filming but it was so much fun that I didn't mind. There's one scene where Jackie hit me five times full in the face, he sweeps me and as I'm going down he hits me in the face with a punch. We were shooting this in really slow motion, so it was obvious that Jackie would be making some contact with me, my body was coming down and his fist was coming up. Because I was facing the

> **"I thought to myself that I'd had so much fun making the film, that I couldn't really believe that I had gotten paid to do it."**

camera, I couldn't wear a mouthpiece and I asked for some cotton wool so that at least I had something to bite on. I told Jackie to hit me once and hit me hard so that we could get the shot. Jackie nodded and we went for it, I dropped and Jackie's fist came up and BOOM! He hit me, but the camera didn't pull back in time to catch the shot right. Jackie asked me if I was okay, I said I was and the camera crew said that their timing was off and we'd have to do the shot again. By the time we did the fifth take, I was having to put ice on my face because it was starting to swell, and the make-up people were having to try and cover up my red face and bruises. I told the camera crew that if they didn't get their timing right this time I was going to hit them! (laughing) "Jackie, this is the last time you're going to hit me, and guys don't make any mistakes this time!" I was ready and so was Jackie, I told him "Give me all you've got! Let's finish this shot!" ACTION! I started to fall and no sooner had I started going down than Jackie's fist came up and it was perfect timing, BOOM! I was used to getting hit but not repeatedly to the face without gloves, I looked over at Jackie and said "I owe you one!" Jackie came up and said thanks to me for being professional and not taking it out on him.

I really enjoyed making the film, and without trying to sound funny, I think that after working on 'Wheels On Meals', I opened a lot of doors for Western martial artists to work in Hong Kong films. The same way I opened the doors for Western fighters to come over to Asia and fight in the ring, I was the first. Before I came over, most Western fighters weren't highly regarded but I changed that.

SP: *A couple of years later, you returned to Hong Kong to film that last Jackie Chan, Samo Hung, Yuen Biao triple header, 'Dragons Forever'. How was that film to work on?*

BU: They called me up and asked me to come back and film another movie. I asked what role I'd be playing and the answer was, "You play bad guy!" (laughing) So I came back and while they still couldn't give me a script, they did give me an outline of the story. I read it and talked to Jackie, and asked him to let me change the style of my fighting for this film and make it more rough and street style. It worked pretty well I thought. We shot the end fight for about three or four days straight, because we really did some nice stuff. I think that Jackie and myself push each other to bring out the best of ourselves when we fight. He knows that he's got to be in the best shape to beat me, and I think that makes our fights work so well.

SP: *Looking back at your work with Jackie, what is your opinion of him?*

BU: I'm a professional fighter, I've fought the best all over the world, that's my job and my life. It's what I do and to meet and work with an actor who is willing to work that hard, and tells me to do my best as I punch and kick is incredible. He's not asking me to come in and beat him up, I always ask Jackie how hard I should be hitting and his answer is always, "Hard, not full strength but enough for a good impact!" And that's what I've been doing, hitting him with good impact but never full power. It's one of the things I most respect about him, I salute the real warrior within him. He has shown me that not only is he a very talented actor and director, but he's also very real. There is a warrior within him and I have been able to bring that warrior out on to the screen. And Jackie knows that I push him to try harder, just as he pushes me.

Basically, Jackie and I gel so well that we're natural. I think of us as real brothers and we just love doing what we're doing. I love working with him because we compliment each other and that brings out the best in both of us. I've worked with him twice, I really enjoyed it and I've learnt a lot and I hope I can work with him again sometime.

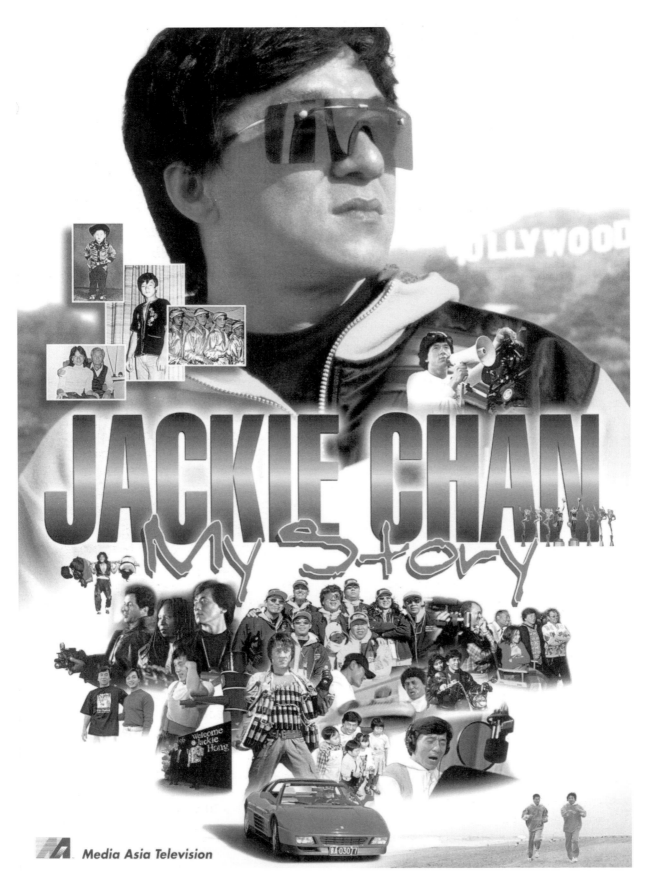

JACKIE CHAN
My Story

Media Asia Television

JACKIE CHAN:
My Story

Reviewed By Gail Mihara

After two years, hundreds of hours of film footage and a tremendous amount of hype, Jackie Chan's much anticipated video autobiography, "My Story", has been released in Asia, with the English version due to hit store shelves during 1998. Designed to introduce Western audiences to the wonders of Jackie, it emerges as a colourful overview of his life and work that's a must for any Chan fan.

English Version

The word to keep in mind here is 'overview'. At a brisk 80 minutes, the documentary is only able to give scant coverage to the many areas it tackles. Samo Hung for example, a major figure in Jackie's life, is only given a minute, Willie Chan not much more. But this approach works well for an audience with only a passing knowledge of Jackie's films and none at all about the man himself.

The highlights of Jackie's life story are covered in the first half of the program, from his birth to Mama and Papa Chan and his tenure at the Peking Opera School to his association with Golden Harvest and current success. The basic areas of interest for new fans are covered as well, such as the kinds of martial arts he practises and his work with Bruce Lee.

Meanwhile, experienced Chan fans will find endless delight in the new interviews as well as some extremely unusual footage. For those searching in vain for Jackie's pre-Lo Wei work, a number of shots are featured from the Lee films as well as a few clean seconds from the vaguely naughty 'All In The Family'.

The real gem, however, is footage of a tiny Jackie in his first film 'Big and Little Wong Tin-bar' (1962). When required, Jackie is pointed out with the aid of hilariously helpful circles and blinking arrows.

Highlights:

- Jackie tells how he learned how to "Bull-S***!" while working as a teenaged stunt director under John Woo. (Essentials: a loud voice and a cigarette.)
- Willie Chan's true role in Jackie's "Discovery" by Lo Wei is set straight.
- Jackie describes the Yugoslavia accident in detail with rare hospital photographs.
- Jackie tells how Spielberg's 'ET' movie gave him a scare while filming 'Project A'.
- Jackie Chan's workout is detailed. (One exercise not to try at home: hang from a bar while a stuntman punches you in the gut like a side of frozen beef!)

Despite its title, 'My Story' remains vaguely detached from its subject for much of its narrator-driven first half. Fortunately the documentary finds its true rhythm 30 minutes in with Jackie's simple statement, "I love cameras". From that moment he takes control of the story and truly makes it his own.

As the English version is designed to introduce Jackie to the Western world, no shocking revelations are contained within. The goal is to make a good first impression and inspire viewers to see more of Jackie's work. The program is not wholly devoid of insight, however. Interview footage where he explains how idle criticism regarding his artistic limitations drove him to make "Miracles" reveals his dedication as a filmmaker. The sight of him wandering around a room next to his office filled with boxes of goods earmarked for charity — including airline giveaway packs Jackie himself has saved — is tangible evidence of his expressed desire to help others. When he speaks honestly about his family life, not only do we get a brief look inside Jackie's modest home, but we also get a brief look inside the man himself.

This is by no means a definitive autobiography, as Jackie is still in his prime. Perhaps in 40 or 50 years when Jackie considers retirement there will be time to consider a more complete and deeper retrospective.

Mandarin Version

If the English version of 'My Story' is a neophyte fan's dream come true, advanced fans will definitely want to check out the Mandarin version, which can be found with subtitles.

Made for the Asian market, the Mandarin version's subject matter is treated very differently from the English version by the filmmakers as well as Jackie himself. The interviews, conducted primarily in Chinese, allow him to express himself in greater detail and with greater feeling, reducing the need for exposition by the narrator.

Though less structured than the English version, the result is a comfortable, confident and effective documentary that manages to tie the experiences of Jackie's past to his current views on film, family, career and the future.

Enlightening interview footage from Chan associates not included in the English version include Emil Chau, Ken Low and Tsui Hark. Even interview clips included in the English version with Sylvester Stallone and Joe Eszterhas run longer in the Mandarin version, providing more insight.

The main benefit of the Mandarin version is that it gives Western fans an opportunity to see another side of their idol, as Jackie sitting in his Hong Kong office is much more thoughtful and serious than the Jackie sitting on David Lettermans's couch. The difference may come as a revelation to non-Asian fans expecting him to be perpetually happy-go-lucky and eager to please.

The documentary's train of thought ends where it began — with Jackie in Hollywood. Though it would seem that he has finally reached the happy ending to his story, it is clear that as far as Jackie Chan is concerned — his story has just begun!

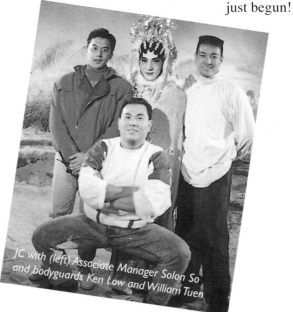

JC with (left) Associate Manager Solon So and bodyguards Ken Low and William Tuen

KENNETH LOW WAI-KWONG

Interviewed
by Mike Leeder

Ken as 'Bobby The Assassin' in Media Asia's '2000 AD'

He's a ring proven kickboxer, but his most memorable fights have been up on the silver screen. He's done battle with the best and the rest, taking on almost all of the biggest names in cinematic martial arts. He did battle with and doubled Brandon Lee in Legacy of Rage, he fought Sonny Chiba protege Shogo Shiyutani in Fighting Fists, he's taken on Jet Lee in My Father the Hero, Yuen Biao in Circus Kids and Donnie Yen in numerous cinematic bouts. He's fought alongside such Hong Kong movie villains as Yu Ring-guong, Dick Wei, Kwan Yeung and Ngai Sing.

Off screen he's Jackie Chan's bodyguard and trusted friend, on screen he's given Jackie a great fight in Thunderbolt, and came the closest anyone has ever come to stealing Jackie's thunder when he unleashed some of the most incredible bootwork committed to celluloid in Drunken Master 2. Now no sooner had he completed work on Jackie's American movie Rush Hour, Ken leapt into production of a swordplay action-adventure show for Hong Kong's ATV network. I caught up with Ken in the early hours of July the 8th for the following skipchat about his life, career and relationship with Jackie.

Screen Power:

Lets begin with some biographical details, where were you born and raised?

Kenneth Low:

I was born in Laos, Cambodia. But when I was fifteen years old, my family fled Cambodia as refugees and relocated to Thailand, and then five years later I came to Hong Kong.

SP: *How did you first get involved with the martial arts?*

KL: I liked fighting when I was a kid. (laughing) When I was at school, my classmates and I would always be fighting, sometimes seriously and sometimes just playing around trying to be Bruce Lee. It wasn't gang fighting; it was one on one. Behind my home there was a Thai Boxing school and the instructors were always asking me to come and join them and study Muay Thai (Thai Boxing) there. I enjoyed training and fighting, but my parents didn't like me fighting and didn't really encourage me or allow me to get too heavily involved.

SP: *You moved from Thailand to Hong Kong when you were twenty. What was the reason for moving here?*

KL: As we've discussed I was a Vietnamese refugee, and at this point, France had agreed to accept so many refugees as permanent residents including myself, and I initially came to Hong Kong on my way to start a new life in France, but I never got there.

SP: *What made you decide to stay in Hong Kong? Was it the chance to work in the local film industry?*

KL: No, it was my mother! (laughing) I was the youngest in my family and despite the fact that I had been offered permanent residency in France, my mother was very worried about me. Everytime I was getting ready to go, she would get very upset, and I ended up deciding to stay.

SP: *When you decided to stay, what did you end up doing for a living?*

KL: I wasn't fighting at that time, I was still training but I hadn't started fighting again. I worked in a kind of hostel for Thai people who were visiting Hong Kong as a kind of Hong Kong tour guide. I would take people around, telling and showing them where to buy things and see things in Hong Kong.

SP: *It was during this period that you started fighting on the Hong Kong circuit. How long did you fight for, and how many professional fights did you have?*

KL: I fought between 1982 and 1984. I only had about seven fights in total. But being a real fighter, I got my chance to work in movies when Tsui Hark was directing a comedy called "Working Class". The film starred Sam Hui (famed singer and former Bruce Lee student), Tsui himself, Teddy Robin and Joey Wong. They wanted Sam to fight a real kickboxer in the movie and I got offered the job, it was three days work for about two minutes of screen time in total, but I liked the feeling of working on a film.

SP: *When and how did you first meet Jackie Chan?*

KL: It was in 1987, I was working as the head of security at one of the top discos here. A lot of film industry people, actors, actresses, directors and producers used to go there including Jackie. And he knew I was doing part time stuntwork in films and invited me to come and work on one of his films, "Project A - Part 2". I did and shortly after this he asked me to stop working at the club, and join his stunt-team, and to become his bodyguard. (laughing) He told me that he could pay me more than the club could, and I decided to take his offer and I've been with Jackie ever since.

SP: *You worked with the late Brandon Lee (Lee Kwok-ho) on "Legacy of Rage", you not only played a featured role as a double gun wielding bad guy, but also as a stunt double.*

KL: I doubled "Daj Sor" (Shing Fui-on) for some of his action scenes, and because at that time Brandon wasn't really much of a martial artist, I doubled him for some action and stunts. Stanley Tong also worked on the film as a stunt double, but Mang Hoi was the stunt/action director for the film.

SP: *How does it feel to be Jackie Chan's bodyguard?*

KL: I feel proud, and I think I must be doing the job okay because I've been with him for more than ten years now. It's taken a long time to learn exactly what Jackie wants. I guess you could say that officially I am still his bodyguard, but I feel that we're so much more than that. We don't have an employer-employee relationship; we are friends with a strong bond.

SP: *Have there been many instances when you've had to defend Jackie?*

KL: Not too many, because Jackie is a very nice guy and I

Ken and fellow JC bodyguard, William Tuen

Ken battles it out with JC in 'Drunken Master 2'

think that almost everybody feels that when they meet him. But there have been times when people want to fight Jackie to prove themselves, they say "Jackie, I want to test you! I want to see if you're real!" I always tell them that they should fight his worst student, me! (laughing) before they fight Jackie!

SP: *In Media Asia's "Jackie Chan: My Story" video you're seen holding the pads for Jackie as the two of you work out. Are you Jackie's personal trainer as well?*

KL: I guess you could say so, we do a lot of martial arts training together, kicking, punching and conditioning training. We do a lot of training together.

SP: *Ken, you're known for your superb kicking ability and flexibility. Has kicking always been something you've been good at, or did you really have to work at it?*

KL: No, I was never very flexible when I started training. I had to work very hard at it from the beginning and I've continued to do so until now, and I think it's paid off. I stretch every day for at least two hours or so, even if I'm just at home watching television, I'll be stretching and keeping limber. To get ready for "Drunken Master 2", I knew Jackie wanted me to be the most flexible I possibly could be so I would stretch out then sit in the splits for two hours or more at a time. This was the first film that working on made me cry!

SP: *How do you keep in such good shape?*

KL: In addition to stretching every day, I do weights for an hour or so, and then I fight the sand bags, punching and kicking to keep my conditioning. Sometimes I do more, sometimes less, depending on my schedule and the films I'm working on.

SP: *You've done a lot of film work outside of Jackie's movies. What's your favourite role and why?*

KL: Hmm, I think my favourite film away from Jackie was an action comedy for Wong Jing. The film was called "Deadly Dream Woman", and starred Chingamy Yau (Yau Suk-ching), Jackie Cheung and Cheung Man. (laughing) It's the one where I'm in the bathrobe with the machine gun! I liked it because I had a chance to act, it was a big role, quite challenging and with some good action. I have very good memories from that film.

SP: *And the worst?*

KL: I don't know the name, it was a Cat 3 film that I did for a producer friend. When I agreed to do the film, I didn't know it was a Cat 3 and the worst thing was they cut me into some sex scenes! The scenes weren't like that when I shot them; they spiced them up in the editing room with additional footage, clever editing and somebody doubling me! I know it's the worst film I've done! It was a long time ago, so hopefully nobody can find it.

SP: *You're most well known for the end fight in "Drunken Master 2", where you and Jackie go toe to toe in one of the best, if not the best, fights in action cinema history. Originally, Ho Sung-pak who originated the role of Lu K'ang in the Mortal Kombat video game was supposed to play the main villain. But you replaced him, can you tell the Screen Power readers how you got the role?*

KL: There were a lot of problems during the making of this film. Ho Sung was supposed to be the main villain, but there were a few problems. One was that he couldn't really catch the rhythm of how we do fight scenes, his timing wouldn't match with ours too well, and also he had to keep flying back to America to do promotion for the video game. So Jackie's original idea was that the end fight would see Ho Sung-pak and me fighting Jackie together. But because Ho Sung-pak wasn't there so much of the time, Jackie and me started playing off each other. Jackie realised just what I could do and I think that inspired him to push to make the fight scene so special and he pushed me up to main villain.

SP: We'll probably get told off for saying this, but it is the closest that anyone's come to stealing a movie from Jackie.

KL: Thank you! A lot of people seem to have enjoyed the fight Jackie and me have, and I am very grateful to Jackie for the chance. Also Jackie wanted to get people very excited, he knows that people are getting bored of too many fight scenes where you know what's going to happen. So for the fight we have, Jackie let me do what I can do best, he let me kick. He made the best use of me in the movie. Jackie needed to make me appear so strong and powerful, he wants you to think that I'm unstoppable and that the only way he can beat me is to get drunk and completely lose control. Of course after Jackie gets drunk, the fight is even more interesting because while I'm still kicking and punching at Jackie, he's doing all this strange dangerous stuff to beat me.

SP: How long did the end fight take to complete?

KL: We worked on the ending pretty much consistently for a month and a half. (laughing) That's incredible, you can't spend that much time on an ending fight scene in America, or even in Hong Kong. Only Jackie can because

people know that it will be worth it! Now so many Hong Kong movies are completed so quickly, that you could finish 4 or 5 movies in the time we shot the fight scene! Too many companies rushing to put out their projects has damaged the Hong Kong film industry.

SP: What do you think of the finished fight scene?

KL: I think that I could do better! At that time I wasn't ready to play such a major role, I wasn't expecting it. I was originally just going to be one of the bad guys, not the main. I didn't have enough time to prepare physically or mentally. That's why I cried during the making of this fight, it was so hard, and I know I could do better. Now if Jackie said to me, we will shoot a big fight scene like this, I'd be ready. I'm prepared now, it got me to train harder and prepare myself more.

SP: You stayed behind the scenes on "Rumble in the Bronx", but stepped in front again as a bootkicking Yakuza hitman in "Thunderbolt". In the pachinko parlour fight scene, you not only lay down some devastating bootwork as yourself, but I'm pretty sure that some of Ken Sewulda's kicks are yours too!

KL: I was training with Jackie every day during

Party time! Jackie throws Ken a birthday surprise on the set of 'Drunken Master 2'

"Rumble", and then I came back for "Thunderbolt". Yes, I did double Ken Sewulda for some of his kicking. He's good but Jackie wanted the kicking to be faster and more furious, also we didn't have a lot of time on this movie. Everything on the film was rush, rush, rush! I've had to double a lot of people working for Jackie. On "City Hunter" I doubled Gary Daniels and Richard Norton for some of their scenes. For a lot of his recent movies, we doubled a lot of the western fighters.

SP: *Of all the Jackie movies you've worked on, which has been the most enjoyable?*

KL: They have all been pretty enjoyable! I have had a lot of fun, and I've learned a lot working with Jackie and so many people on these films. I like the films where we've gone abroad to film, I get to see the world, the money's better! (laughing) Outside of Hong Kong I don't have so much pressure, people don't know me, and don't have this idea of how I should behave or how they should treat me. I like it. It's nice sometimes to not have everybody know who you are.

SP: *Jackie's most recent movie is "Rush Hour", his first movie with New Line Cinema. The film's directed by Brett Ratner and sees Jackie co-starring with Chris Tucker in his first American production since "The Protector" way back. What role do you play in the film, and how was it working on a big Hollywood production for the first time?*

KL: I play a Chinese killer, and I get to fight Jackie and Chris Tucker this time. It was very funny fighting Chris because he was very worried about getting hit by me and some of the other stunt-team. For one scene, I'm meant to be standing really close to Chris, face to face, but I kick him in the head. He didn't believe that I could hit him from so close, until Jackie got me to demonstrate. (laughing) But you have less real contact doing the fight scenes, you have to stop short and bring back. Jackie and the rest of the JC Stuntmen's Club took care of the action scenes featuring Chris Tucker. I think what made Jackie frustrated was that the insurance company and the studio held Jackie back from doing too many dangerous stunts, Jackie felt dissatisfied with being held back so much. I know the director was very worried

about Jackie, he kept saying that he didn't want to be the director who hurt or killed Jackie Chan. He was afraid that if anything happened to Jackie, everybody would want to kill him! But working in America was a lot easier than working in Hong Kong. It feels very comfortable, there's a buffet every day, the working hours are much shorter. The technical knowledge and skill of the American crew is very good, they have much more scientific ways of doing things, they are more specialised whereas in Hong Kong you're expected to be able to do everything or somebody else will take your place. Their safety precautions are better, the stunts are adjusted money wise, the more dangerous the stunt the higher the pay. In Hong Kong, if you're a stuntman everybody expects you to just do it and the salary is much lower.

SP: *If the chance to do more work in the West comes up, would you be interested?*

KL: Yes, a few companies have approached me about a couple of projects but so far nothing is definite. It's all just talking at the moment.

SP: *You've worked so closely with Jackie for so long, and you know him so well. Can you describe to the Screen Power readers the way you see the relationship between the two of you?*

KL: As I already said, it's not just an employer-employee relationship. Even at the beginning I felt close to Jackie, and over all this time, we've become very close friends, and I regard and think of Jackie as my brother. Jackie doesn't tell me that I must go with him and follow him here and there, we go together as friends, and it's no longer a job to me. The bond between us is very strong. I am very grateful to Jackie for giving me so many opportunities and so much support.

SP: *Away from filming and training, what does Ken Low do to relax?*

KL: I watch a lot of movies, go swimming. I do most of the things that everybody else does.

SP: *Well good luck with everything, Ken, and thanks for taking the time to talk to us. It has been a great pleasure.*

KL: Thank you! It was fun!

An Alan Smithee Film
Burn Hollywood Burn

Directed by:	*Alan Smithee*
Written by:	*Joe Eszterhas*
Starring:	*Eric Idle, Ryan O'Neal and Richard Jeni*
With Special Appearances by:	*Jackie Chan, Whoopi Goldberg and Sylvester Stallone*

Reviewed By: Gail Mihara

Photos courtesy of BEN MYRON PRODUCTIONS (USA)

Note: When a movie is tampered with by powers beyond a director's control, the director can apply for a Smithee. This option allows the fictional Alan Smithee to take credit — or blame — for a film that might otherwise taint an actual person's resume.

November 1996 cameras rolled on "An Alan Smithee Film", the latest project from bad boy millionaire screenwriter Joe Eszterhas. Helmed by "Love Story" director Arthur Hiller, the film boasted an impressive trio of big star cameos: Sylvester Stallone, Whoopi Goldberg, and Jackie Chan in his first Hollywood role since 1985's "The Protector". Industry trade papers were abuzz with news of the upcoming blockbuster — a smart, sardonic satire of the insanity that is Hollywood.

What a difference a year and a half makes.

By May 1997 Arthur Hiller had removed his name from the Hollywood Pictures project after bad test audience reactions inspired Eszterhas to slash 22 minutes from the film. As a result, "An Alan Smithee Film" became an Alan Smithee film.

Then the actors turned on the movie: Sylvester Stallone publicly dismissed the film, expressing the desire to take a Smithee himself. The film's star, Eric "Nudge Nudge" Idle, declared it "A mess". Even Eszterhas seemed to sense impending doom and cancelled all pre-release interviews, citing throat problems. The studio's attitude towards the film was reflected in the graphic of its nondescript print ad—an anonymous brown paper package wrapped in twine.

On 27th February 1998 Hollywood Pictures swept the newly titled "An Alan Smithee Film Burn Hollywood Burn" under the rug of a few token theatres, as if hoping it might go unnoticed. It did not, as critics had a field day describing it as, among other things, "spectacularly bad", "wretched", "bilious", and, courtesy of USA Today, "a huge, steaming pile".

But how bad is it, really? In three words — pretty darn bad.

"Burn Hollywood Burn" chronicles the trials and tribulations of a first time director at the helm of "Trio", the most expensive action blockbuster ever made. Problems arise when meddling by the film's producer renders it so bilious that it is unfit for public consumption. The director would take a Smithee but his name really is Alan Smithee. What to do?

Simple — steal the movie.

The filming and theft of "Trio" is chronicled mock-documentary style, with on camera commentary from various characters about the film, Hollywood, themselves, or something else entirely. Smithee, locked up in a mental institution after the theft, relates how his film was corrupted and prostituted. Producer/corrupter James Edmunds (Ryan O'Neal) denies all charges, insisting he is a producer, not a pimp ("There's a difference!").

Meanwhile, the film's stars — the stars of "Trio", that is — have their own agendas. As Stallone pontificates about the redemption of his character in the film, a cigar-chomping Goldberg and an adamant Jackie make it clear their characters are not going to die if Stallone's doesn't. "No die! No die! No die!" Jackie declares.

Instead of a sly take on the film industry, "Burn Hollywood Burn" is actually Joe Eszterhas's revenge fantasy — ninety minutes of mean-spirited verbal spitballs aimed at everything he thinks is wrong with Hollywood. Fun for him, but not much for the audience.

Eszterhas does little to tailor the script for Jackie beyond removing all references to his first choice, Bruce Willis. While Stallone and Goldberg are given ample opportunity to poke fun at their world famous public personas, Jackie's role is fairly generic. Nevertheless, he makes the most of what he's given and turns in an interesting performance as a slightly daffy, sublimely self-centred superstar who talks about reincarnation and knocks the heads off wooden kung fu dummies to make his point.

Ironically, there is more "Smithee" footage in "My Story" than there is of Jackie in "Smithee" itself. His screen time is approximately two minutes, with footage sprinkled in the begining, middle and end of the movie. A flubbed take plays during the end credits, but unfortunately even this movie's out-takes stink.

The main benefit of "Burn Hollywood Burn" is that Jackie's participation confirms his status in Hollywood as a major star. As a film, however, it emerges as little more than a minor curiosity in the "Cannonball Run" and "Killer Meteor" vein. It's like watching paint dry.

For Jackie's real return to Hollywood, best wait for "Rush Hour".

Scene by scene:

What follows is every single line of dialogue Jackie has in this film. No fooling.

Scene 1: On the set of "Trio", the star trio films a scene where each fires a shotgun into the camera, yelling "Don't f*%k with me!" The take is completed, but an uncertain Smithee suggests another try. The stars, however, insist they nailed it. "Nailed it! Nailed it!" Jackie says with irritation. His friend Stallone is more direct: "If you don't get that camera out of my face, I'm gonna Sean Penn your ass!"

Scene 2: Jackie is surrounded by suits at a studio meeting. He is not pleased by the news that his character will be killed off instead of Stallone's: "No! I will not die! I will absolutely not die. Positively not die. No die, no die, no die!"

Scene 3: Later at that same meeting, Jackie explains a few things: "I cannot die. I never die. Even if I die, I will come back with reincarnation. So I never die. OK?" A studio man gives him the thumbs-up sign. Jackie is pleased.

Scene 4: Jackie, decked out in a gi, turns his satisfaction into a workout chant: "Good! Good! No die! Good! No die! No reincarnation! Good! Good! No die!"

Scene 5: Standing next to a wooden kung fu dummy, Jackie explains his relationship with directors: "The director is in control of everything. But he is not in control of me. As long as he's not in control of me, I help the director be in control. If somehow he stupidly thinks he's in control of me..." To literally drive his point home, Jackie punches the head off the dummy.

Scene 6: Everyone is clamouring to play the lead in the upcoming movie about Smithee, Jackie included. As he lounges in the back of a limo full of lissome Asian women, he explains why he should get the part: "Yes. He's an action hero. He wins. He's just like me. He kills everybody. I kill everybody. So, we're brothers!"

Scene 7: Jackie does more damage back at the gym as he decapitates another dummy while explaining his next step in snagging the Smithee role: "I'll call my agent!"

JC, Stallone and Goldberg in 'An Alan Smithee Film'

RUSH HOUR
Review

by Gail Mihara

(Movie images courtesy of Ileen Reich of New Line Cinema)

In 1985 a disastrous film known as "The Protector" accomplished something that twisted limbs, cracked ribs and a hole in the head couldn't do — it caused Jackie Chan to give up. The failure of that film led him to write off the American market and leave Hollywood, vowing never to return. He did return, of course, in 1996 with the release of "Rumble in the Bronx". However, despite this and subsequent successes, Jackie has yet to become a household name. No doubt that will change in light of the $33 million opening of his first American film in over a decade, "Rush Hour".

While surprising, the film's phenomenal box-office success is more than justified. "Rush Hour" is a joyful, funny action romp that salvages a tepid summer movie season cluttered with such overblown would-be blockbusters as "Godzilla" and "The Avengers".

Jackie plays Inspector Lee, a top Hong Kong cop who busts the operation of Juntao, a vicious crime lord. Like any good villain, Juntao escapes Jackie's justice with notions of vengeance on all those who opposed him, including Inspector Lee's close ally, the Chinese Consul Han (Tzi Ma).

During a diplomatic mission to the United States, Han's daughter (Julie Hsu) is kidnapped. Despite assurances from the authorities that they will find the kidnappers and return his daughter safely, the distraught father calls on Inspector Lee for help.

The FBI, in turn, calls on LAPD detective James Carter (Chris Tucker) to keep Lee from meddling in the case. Carter, the type of irreverant movie cop who blows stuff up between jokes, has his own plan to find and rescue Han's daughter. This plan,

JC hangs around in downtown LA

however, does not include Lee, and the LA cop tries his best to encourage the Hong Kong cop to do some sightseeing instead.

Inspector Lee has other ideas and barges his way into the middle of the investigation, much to the dismay of both Carter and the Feds.

Shut out by the FBI, Lee and Carter decide to team up and crack the case themselves. It becomes a race against time to find the little girl before Juntao's revenge can be exacted or the FBI sends Lee's sorry ass back to Hong Kong.

"Rush Hour" is a buddy cop film and proud of it. All the classic elements are honoured: the mismatched, bickering protagonists who eventually learn to respect each other; the disapproving police chief; the bonding sequence where the two cops compare scares and get drunk, etc. Luckily for the audience, director Brett Ratner is smart enough to take these clichés and give everything a fresh twist to keep things new.

Also given a fresh twist is Jackie's own screen persona, which is a distinct departure from his usual good-natured everyman in jeopardy. Gone are the shaggy haircut, sneakers and baggy sweatshirts of old. Instead he is a confident veteran, a leader of men in a killer suit and sleek haircut. (And he looks fantabulous, baby.)

Besides the sneakers, also missing are the extended fight sequences, something that will surely vex some fans. Fortunately, while the fight scenes are not nearly as long as they are in Hong Kong, the comedy and character interaction more than make up for it. Fight-wise, Jackie still manages to deliver the goods, such as in the climactic sequences where he bashes the bad guys while trying to prevent a wavering, gargantuan antique vase from toppling over.

Another deviation from the norm is the presence of an equal partner for Jackie in the form of Chris Tucker. Deemed "The Next Big Thing" by no less than Newsweek magazine, Tucker has taken the fast track from stand-up stage to feature films in the span of a few short years. "Rush Hour" marks his debut as an A-list headliner, providing high powered, in-your-face comic relief in contrast with Jackie's relatively laid-back, softer-edged humour. Reportedly Tucker is getting a whopping $7 million for his next flick, "Double-O-Soul". But is he worth it?

Jackie and co-star Chris Tucker

The answer: "Yes". With Jackie taking on the bulk of the physical duties, Tucker pulls his weight by providing a non-stop barrage of stand-up schtick. Every situation is an opportunity for him to launch into a riff, much to Jackie's on-screen (and, reportedly, off-screen) bewilderment. This makes Tucker a lot of fun to watch, with his comedic indignance, chutzpah and patented "happy dance" when things go his way.

The chemistry and comedic friction between Tucker and Jackie is comfortable and playful throughout, though it seems even more joyous during the outtakes. Their personalities also manage to compliment their characters, with Tucker playing the ambitious young rookie who makes a great noise to get attention and impress everyone, while Jackie is the self-assured veteran who watches, bemused, then does his own thing. Indeed, Jackie is the soul of the film, delivering the material with such integrity and sincerity that the audience grows to care about what's happening to the characters. When Lee is being sent back to Hong Kong after failing to retrieve the little girl, his despair at having failed her is palpable and lends the necessary

humanity a film like this so desperately needs.

Ultimately the relationship between the two men is the true featured attraction of this film. A male bonding scene where Carter seeks to funk up Lee's rendition of the classic soul song "War" tickles the audience even more than the big explosions and action set pieces.

Among a fine supporting cast a real standout is Julia Hsu as Han's daughter. A first time actress, Hsu is unaffected and adorable as the spunky kidnap victim and Inspector Lee's kung fu pupil and friend. "Don't forget to practise your eye gouges," he reminds her. Their scenes together are charming and full of heart.

"Rush Hour" is entertaining fun and a welcome relief from the violent and humourless action fare currently being churned out by the major studios. An excellent cast raises the material to a higher level and there are plenty of delightful surprises to be found for both fans and general audiences alike.

Jackie Chan has definitely arrived in America. Again. And with the blockbuster success of "Rush Hour", this time he's here to stay.

RUSH HOUR DVD

By Myra Bronstein, Jeanne Fredriksen, Liz Langley and Gail Mihara

全米No.1! オープニング記録樹立!!
早くも全米興収160億円突破!

今、世界で一番面白い映画がやってくる!!

クリス・タッカー ジャッキー・チェン

ラッシュアワー
RUSH HOUR

ブレット・ラトナー監督作品
「セブン」「マスク」のニュー・ライン・シネマ製作

98年秋、
全米で一番ヒットした映画!

「タイタニック」
「プライベート・ライアン」を超える
オープニング成績!

「セブン」「マスク」を超える
ニュー・ライン・シネマ
歴代No.1!

サントラCD
全米ビルボード第4位!

主題歌
「HOW DEEP IS YOUR LOVE」
by Dru Hill
全米ビルボード第1位!

Japanese promotional material for 'Rush Hour'

Features:

The opening/main page has a "vamp til ready" scene and music while you decide what to choose. The scene is Chan and Tucker in the car, with Tucker doing his "snake dance" and Jackie doing the double takes.

Choices Are:
* Play Movie

* Language Selections:
- *English 5.1 Surround Sound*
- *English Stereo Surround Sound*
- *English subtitles (on/off)*

* Special Features:
- *Audio commentary by director Brett Ratner.* The film audio is faint beneath Brett's monologue and the audio increases when he pauses between explanations.
- *Isolated score with commentary by composer Lalo Schifin.* No dialogue from the film is heard behind the music or commentary.

* Deleted Scenes:
- *Soo Yung late for school*
- *Pool room*
- *Leaving the Consulate/Being rebuffed by the FBI*
- *Carter retrieves the corvette outside the Consulate*
- *Pick up Johnson before exhibition*
- *Lee, Carter and Johnson crash the exhibition*
- *"Are you on the list?"*

* A Piece Of The Action:
Behind the Scenes of Rush Hour. This is the entry point for the fantastic footage to follow.

Getting With Jackie:
Brett Ratner (Director) and Roger Birnbaum (Producer) describe flying to South Africa for one day to woo Jackie for "Rush Hour".

Working With Chris:
Brett and Chris Tucker give their differing accounts

of how Chris joined the cast.

Brett Ratner - Action Star:
Brett tries vainly to perform the same, seemingly easy, feats of co-ordination as Jackie—with arms, legs, squares, and circles.

Chris Tucker - Action Star:
Chris tries vainly to perform the same, seemingly easy, feats of co-ordination as Jackie—this time with coins. A pattern emerges.

Brett Ratner - Energy, Detail, Personality:
Brett's directing skill is analysed, and attributed by Chris to the atypical existence of personality in a director.

Hard At Work:
Brett fine-tunes Jackie and Chris' performances in a variety of scenes.

Intimidating The Director:
Elizabeth Pena describes playing bawdy body pranks on Brett.

Oh, The Chemistry:
Cast and crew shenanigans illustrate the fun on the "Rush Hour" set.

Fights... Fireworks... And Brett's Mama:
Chris plays at trash talking Brett.

Doubts When Shooting:
Cast and crew assess scenes.

The Hardest Part Of Acting:
Jackie articulates his trouble with dialogue; Chris ad-libs scenes to Jackie's consternation.

Jackie's Stunts:
Brett and Terry Leonard (Stunt Co-ordinator) tell how they keep the stunts—and Jackie—safe.

Buster Keaton And Musicals:
Jackie cites Buster Keaton and Gene Kelly as major influences.

A Piece Of The Action:
DVD pay dirt. Jackie choreographs and rehearses the restaurant fight with energy and imagination and athleticism. We get to see how his amazing stuntmen must read his agile mind and mirror his lightning fast movements to help demonstrate his concept for an action scene. It's the best footage on

JC kicks out in New Line's 'Rush Hour'

the best disc. And a big treat for any Jackie fan.

Outtakes And In Jokes/Credits:

Additional outtakes are shown.

* *Original Theatrical Trailer*

* *Cast & Crew Credits*

This section has bios and filmographies for Tucker, Chan, Wilkinson, Pena, Julia Hsu and Tzi Ma under Cast. For Jackie, they have separate listings for Film Filmography, Director Filmography, Writer Filmography, Producer Filmography, and Misc. Crew Filmography. The Crew Credits talk about everyone from Brett Ratner and Lalo Schifrin to the Producers, the Screenwriters, the Directors of Photography, Costume Designer, Film Editor.

* *Short Film: Brett Ratner's Student Film, "What Ever Happened To Mason Reese"*

* *Music Video: "Nuttin' But Love" by Heavy D*

* *Music Video: "How Deep Is Your Love" by Dru Hill*

* *Scene Selections - 37 chapters on the disc.*

Note: Both videos offer the director's (Ratner's) commentary if desired.

DVD-ROM material includes:

* *"Find the Ambassador's Daughter" game, which is hard to figure out, but winners are congratulated by Brett Ratner, then "rewarded" with an Easter Egg. The Easter Egg is yet another of Ratner's early short films, this one called "Evil Luke Lee".*

* *"Say What" timed game, in which player matches movie dialogue to movie characters and answers related trivia questions.*

* *Script to screen capability, which claims to have the latest version. Like the published script sold individually by New Line, it doesn't match the final dialogue at all.*

* *Lots of still photos from the movie.*

* *More bio and plot synopsis material.*

* *Web tie ins.*

* *New Line promos.*

Although to many die hard Jackie Chan fans "Rush Hour" was something of a disappointment as it didn't really allow Jackie to let loose, the film did incredible business at both the American and International Box Office and confirmed Jackie's rightful place as an international action movie star.

"Rush Hour 2" started production in December 2000 in Los Angeles. The film will reunite Chan with co-star Chris Tucker and director Brett Ratner. The film will be shot on location in Hong Kong and the USA.

JC poses for photos at the LA Premiere of 'Rush Hour'

SAMMO HUNG

The Martial Law Interview

SCREEN POWER'S "US CORRESPONDENT"
RENEE WITTERSTAETTER TALKS TO
SAMMO HUNG ON THE L.A. SET OF CBS'S NEW
ACTION TELEVISION SERIES, "MARTIAL LAW"

Screen Power:

Sammo, you're a huge star in Hong Kong and other parts of the world. This is your first television show in the United States... so, just for some background if someone is discovering you and your films for the first time, what are your favourites?

Sammo Hung:

What's my favourite? Some movies that are my favourite ones are 'Prodigal Son' and 'Eastern Condors' and 'Heart of Dragon'. I like those.

SP: *'Prodigal Son' was with Yuen Biao, one of your Peking Opera School brothers?*

SH: Yes, Yuen Biao.

SP: *A wonderful movie. Everyone should check that one out.*

SH: (laughing) Ah Yes! Another one is 'Pedicab Driver'. I like that one too...

SP: *And 'Close Encounters of the Spooky Kind'? I know that is a favourite of a lot of people.*

SH: Uh huh...

SP: *Now, I heard that 'Close Encounters of the Spooky Kind' was inspired by actual spiritual tales that your Mother told you as a child.*

SH: Some. But mostly the basis was from what my master told me at the Peking Opera School. I didn't know if it was true or not true, you know, but he told me they were true stories. I heard all these true stories from my master. My master, he had lived in Beijing—the old village—and there were a lot of stories about ghosts and everything.

SP: *You grew up with the same master in the same Peking Opera School as Jackie Chan and Yuen Biao as I mentioned. Some people may not know that.*

SH: Yes, Yes.

SP: *Was it your choice to go there? And how many years did you stay there?*

SH: First, it was not my choice. Well, half was my choice because the first time my friends asked my Grandpop "Why don't you bring Sammo to the Peking Opera School? Then he can really learn something." You can tell I really didn't like a normal school. The street when I was 8 or 9 years old was bad... then after my friends introduced me to the Peking Opera School, I felt it was interesting. I told my friends I wanted to enter the school. Then I signed a contract to stay there seven years.

SP: *Seven years? For the readers that don't know, this was a school that taught martial arts, acrobatics and tradition Peking Opera.*

SH: Yes.

SP: *There was a movie about your time there called 'Painted Faces'...*

SH: Yes.

SP: *Is it close to the reality?*

SH: Half and half.

SP: *Really?*

SH: Yeah. On the school scenes, some things are very true, but there are other things with the love story—too fancy!

SP: *I heard Jackie say it was a very tough existence?*

SH: Yeah, yeah, Jackie's right. Very tough.

SP: *Where did you learn how to choreograph? You are very well known for your splendid choreography.*

SH: When I was 16 years old, I was leaving school, and my job was... I had been a stuntman, and I was very interested in movies for the fighting and everything. I just learn, learn, learn. I work with this director and that director. I work with this action director and that action director.

SP: *Tell me about 'Martial Law'. How did this series come about?*

SH: Because I was thinking of retiring from acting, you know. So a few years go by, then my friends told me I should stick with the acting. "It's not hard... it's fun." Okay, so I say, "Let me think about it." At first I think about never acting again, you know. And acting again as a main character... It was mainly interesting for me to be directing at this point. So, Stanley Tong, he

BANG! *Sammo hits out!*

called me and told me about the character and it was very good. I like the character. So, okay, I did it.

SP: *What did you like about the character so much that it drew you back into acting?*

SH: I like the character because I saw a lot of movies where the Chinese characters were not different from each other—not like in Hong Kong movies. My character comes from Shanghai, he is a Policeman and he's very strict, very serious, and he's very human. You know—very human? Just like he belonged to me. So, I really liked the character. I like to build the character. With the character, I can show something. Show something of the Chinese culture, the American culture—the difference. The Chinese Police have a very different type of Father, Mother, Grandmother, children. I do not think this is always good. We are all different. On this show, I grew up in China, they grew up in America, we are supposed to have different cultures. So, the Los Angeles Police Department may do something one way, and I may do something different. They will have a way of doing things in the United States that I don't do. Of course, it's very funny and a lot of fun.

SP: *How does it feel doing a television show as opposed to doing a movie? Usually you have complete control over your movies.*

SH: For the first time, I'm just acting. Because I don't have time to care about producing or the production, everything, because one of the things I really need to do is learn English. This is very important to me, and I'm shooting everyday, so I don't have time to create any stories, any scenes. I love to... Sometimes I'd love to be directing an episode. But I don't have time. One thing that is very different for me is when shooting a movie I have a lot of time. I can set everything up and if today we don't finish, tomorrow we can go on. Continue. On television everything just moves very fast. The fighting—you must finish today, not tomorrow. Seven days for one episode. It's very different from movies. Here one fighting scene can take months. It's a very, very... I'm still learning how... we put each episode together, maybe two scenes, maybe three scenes for fighting and only in eight days! I'm learning how to do all this! (laughing)

SP: *I'm sure you give advice with all your wealth of experience.*

SH: A little...

SP: *Have you ever worked with Stanley Tong before?*

SH: No.

SP: *No? How is it going?*

SH: It's okay.

SP: *Really. He'll never see this!*

SH: (laughing) He's really working very hard. He's doing so many things. Very good.

SP: *Your time slot is right before 'Walker Texas Ranger'.*

SH: Uh huh...

SP: *Which is a very strong position. What do you think of Chuck Norris personally?*

SH: Hmmm... I think Chuck Norris is good because he shows a totally different type of story on his show. The tone is different. Everything is different. But, I think Chuck is very good.

SP: *He fought Bruce Lee in one of his movies, which is still considered one of the best on screen martial arts fights of all time. But, I know you've had a few run-ins with Bruce Lee yourself off screen in real life. Can you tell us about that?*

SH: Huh... The first time I met Bruce Lee, I had heard about him, you know?

SP: *Yeah.*

SH: He didn't know me. Then I'm shooting on the set, and he just came to visit my set and somebody introduced us. "This is Bruce Lee. This is Sammo." Then I was very young, just 19 or 20 years old. Then I asked him, "You're the Bruce Lee?" "Yes." "Are you really fast?" "So what? What do you want to do?" I said, "I don't know." I'm just watching him. He said, "You want to try?" I said, "Why not!"

SP: *No?*

SH: Then we are both standing on the set. I tried to do something. He tried to do something. Before I knew what had happened—before I could move—he had kicked me in the face!

SP: *Oh my goodness!*

SH: POW!!! Just like that. His foot is still in front of my face, and he says "How do you feel?" I said,

"You're very good!" (laughing) What else could I say? It's true!

SP: *Oh, that's great!*

SH: After this, we became good friends, all the time talking, talking. Then, he started 'Game of Death' and told me he had a great character for me. I said, "Okay, no problem." Then I'm waiting for a year or so, then nobody tell me anything. "I need a job, you know!" I told him. Of course, I get a job shooting with another director. I went to Bangkok for shooting. Then they started 'Game of Death'. When they started 'Enter the Dragon' he called me, "Hey, I want to fight with you in the beginning scene. In two days." I said, "How can I do that? I'm shooting everyday in Bangkok." I went to Hong Kong. Just back two days. Got my shooting done in two days. Then went back to Bangkok.

SP: *Then I heard you had to come back and do a fill in scene on 'Game of Death' after Bruce Lee died?*

SH: Yeah, after he died.

SP: *So you two did work together a little bit?*

SH: A little bit. But we had a good time when I came back to Hong Kong and we were shooting in the studio and he came every day. We'd go to his office and he'd show me everything—the guns, the weapons, everything. We'd talk about the WuShu and martial arts—what were the good ones. How did you use the weapon, how did you catch the weapon. You know? We'd talk about everything. Every time we'd talk like that. Yeah.

SP: *Some of my favourite movies that you've done were 'Project A' and 'Dragons Forever'. Where the three brothers appeared together— you, Yuen Biao and Jackie Chan. That was magic. Do you think we'll ever see some guest stars on 'Martial Law' like that?*

SH: I think this is possible. I hope 'Martial Law' is successful then we'll try to get Yuen Biao and other guest stars. Yeah. It's a good idea. I really want to. We may try to do it.

SP: *Do you want to direct some episodes?*

SH: I want to, but I'm still thinking about how I can make it in eight days.

SP: *Yeah.*

SH: Because I still want some good fight scenes, good action that's in my style, of course I want to show something. But, I'm still learning.

SP: *The trailers look good. I sort of like this Sammo Hung punching bag too. Can I get one? (Editors note: A smaller than life size punching bag of Sammo is prominent in the office.)*

SH: I leave it here in the office, everyone punches me. (laughing)

SP: *(Laughing) Thanks so much Sammo for the interview.*

SH: You're welcome.

SP: *And you know, your English is already good because you understand my Texas accent.*

SH: Thank you! You give me a chance to learn more English!

SP: *Good luck!*

Factoids:

Martial Law ran for two seasons on CBS. Upon its completion Sammo returned to Hong Kong to appear in Andrew Lau's Legend of the Iron Fist. He is currently shooting Time's Up, for B & S Creations about a Buddhist monk who must battle terrorists in Hong Kong and China. Hung is also set to make his international directorial debut in the very near future with a live action adaptation of a popular video game.

Martial Law featured former Jackie Chan stunt-teamer Andy Cheng as one of its primary choreographers, along with Jackie and Sammo's Peking Opera classmate Richard Hung (Yuen Tak).

This guy gets top billing.

I AM
JACKIE
CHAN
My Life in Action
JACKIE CHAN

A Ballantine Hardcover
September 1998

Interview by Gail Mihara

"Written with verve and narrative skill by Jeff Yang... ["I Am Jackie Chan"] is as funny, brisk and exciting as any Jackie movie, with the surprise of poignancy."
Richard Corliss, Time Magazine

When word got out that Ballantine had acquired the rights to Jackie Chan's autobiography, fans were simultaneously ecstatic and alarmed. Ecstatic because they were finally going to hear the real story from the man himself. Alarmed because the man himself would have a co-writer: Jeff Yang.

Some were concerned that the 'Yang Factor' might somehow distort or dilute the tale Jackie wanted to tell. Others worried that the narrative voice would be Jeff's rather than Jackie's. Fortunately the final product, "I Am Jackie Chan", is a fascinating and poignant account of an extraordinary life, told in a voice that is distinctly Jackie's.

Great curiosity remains, however, about Jackie's somewhat mysterious collaborator. Heeding the call, Screen Power went directly to the source and now answers the question that has been niggling at fans for months:

Just who is Jeff Yang?

Jeff Yang's journey into Chan country began in 1989. Fresh out of Harvard University, he and three friends sat down and decided to launch one of the first publications aimed specifically at English-speaking Asian Americans: A. Magazine: Inside Asian America. Besides addressing the relevant issues of this previously overlooked community, the young entrepreneurs also hoped to take advantage of what they sensed would be an emerging influence of Asian Culture on the national consciousness.

Building on this cultural shift, A. Magazine would, under Yang's guiding hand, eventually grow to boast a circulation of 180,000. Not only that, but as the media's designated expert on Asian American issues, Yang increasingly found himself being consulted on a variety of topics both important and obscure. After receiving one too many requests to give his opinion on Asia's spiciest cuisine, he decided to put together his first book.

The result was "Eastern Standard Time", an encyclopaedia of Asian American pop-culture hors d'oeuvres of information cooked up by the A. Magazine staff. One section in particular gave significant coverage to Hong Kong cinema and its principle players, including a certain actor/director/producer/stuntman/etc...

As often happens in life, one thing leads to another,

and the success of "Eastern Standard Time" soon brought Yang a call from a stranger with a mysterious proposition...

JEFF YANG:

Shortly after the book was published in May 1997, I got a call from an agent named Ling Lucas with a very obscure proposal. She called me up and said, "I have a project that I think you'd be perfect for, but I can't tell you what it is." And I said, "If you can't tell me what it is, I can't tell you if I'm perfect for it." [But] I said, "All right, I'll go to the meeting."

The meeting was with Peter Borland and Judith Curr. Judith is the editor in chief of Ballantine, Peter Borland is the executive editor there. I asked, "What's this big project you're working on?" Judith said in a very quaint Australian accent that they had picked up the rights to Jackie Chan's autobiography.

I had heard the rumour that Jackie was doing his autobiography, just from other sources, and the figures that were being thrown around for what they were paying him were pretty enormous. But whatever the number, I never found out. All I know is, I didn't get paid that much! I got paid very well, but the numbers that they were tossing around were movie star numbers. And to me that meant something big, because as big as Jackie is around the world, in America he's always been seen as a second class citizen. Well, I knew different just from observing the reaction we've gotten to "Eastern Standard Time" and the letters and e-mails we received at A. Magazine. I knew that as big a star as he was internationally, he was a superstar in the making in America.

Besides which, I grew up on Jackie Chan and the Shaw Brothers. As soon as they said it was Jackie Chan's biography and that they needed somebody to work with him, the man himself, I said, "Where do I sign?"

And I guess the rest is a little bit of history.

SCREEN POWER:

Before meeting Jackie, did you have any

preconceived notions about what he would be like?

JY: I'd heard from everybody that he was one of the nicest guys you'll ever meet. But to tell you the truth, I wasn't sure what I would think of him as a person as opposed to as a personality. And part of it is he's always on. If you watch him in movies, if you see him in interviews, it's always Jackie.

SP: "Jackie"—with quotation marks.

JY: Exactly. Maybe with a capital J-A-C-K-I-E. The reality is, I've met people who are "stars"

Jackie's Official Autobiography - have you got your copy yet?

before, and most of them, behind the scenes— no matter how charming and affable and sweet they are on screen—you meet them in person and you're primed for disappointment. Because people are people. Well, I was both pleasantly shocked and also surprised to find that Jackie in person is every bit as warm and good-natured and just as lovely a human being as he appears to be. The added plus, especially for an autobiographer, is that he's a lot more complex than he lets on.

He's been making movies and performing since he was seven, eight years old and as an adult, now that he's kind of created—well, if it ain't broke, don't fix it. So the Jackie you see is the Jackie who repeats the same things again and again. The Jackie who always has exactly the right quip for the questions he's going to be asked and never talks about aspects of himself that he knows his fans don't want to hear. Well, he's actually somebody who has a lot of depth. And a lot of intellect. Both street smarts and, really, wisdom. In a way that isn't obvious from his 'clown prince' persona.

SP: Do you have any examples of that?

JY: I think the most self-evident thing, once you actually get to sit down and talk with him— this is for the complexity aspect—is that for all that he is somebody who has such great achievements and who, especially when he's with his fans, is tremendously happy... he's somebody who has a lot of sadness in his life. [He] has been driven by inner demons that have kind of put him in the position of succeeding, almost in spite of himself. If you see him on movie sets, [he's] happy-go-lucky Jackie one instant, joking with his stuntmen, breaking up the whole crew... a few minutes later he'll be hunched down in his director's chair, with his parka pulled over his head, staring off into the distance and you don't know what he's staring at. Maybe at his own mortality? Maybe at a lifetime which has never been easy, even at its best. Maybe it's the ghosts that have surrounded him. More so now than ever with the deaths of some of the people who were most instrumental in changing his life.

When you're talking about the standard stuff, he gives the standard Jackie answer. But when you start peeling back some of the scabs... I've seen him on the verge of tears, I've seen his eyes flash with anger, I've seen him scared. And scared not just of physical feats, like stunts that could kill him, but scared, in some ways, of really confronting some of the stuff that he's had to do to get where he is, and some of the stuff that people in his life have sacrificed in order to enable him to be who he is.

SP: *While on that subject, Jackie is a very private person. How did you get him to open up?*

JY: The biggest part of this project wasn't actually just sitting down and talking with Jackie, it was almost becoming a part of Jackie's circle. I mean, I can't say that I'm an intimate of his.

SP: *He does have certain people who travel with him and that he's very close to.*

JY: Having those people there in some cases and talking to those people, and knowing what the questions are to ask, that helped a lot. Talking to people like Ken [Low], talking to his stuntmen, talking to Willie, talking to his assistants like Osumi... They've seen him at his best and worst. They also know the hidden little bits of him that flash once in a while. I told Jackie and Willie and Judith and Peter that if I was going into this, as much as I am a fan of Jackie's, I couldn't do it as a Jackie fan. I had to do it as Jackie. I had to be as driven and, in some cases, even as cruel as one needs to be in order to peel back the outer shell of somebody who's lived for decades with a shell.

I actually probed the people around him, asking for points where they've seen him weak or vulnerable or unsure of himself. Not so that I could ask him a question that would hurt him, but because I knew those were the points where he would have to talk. He doesn't talk about his family. He doesn't talk about the real anecdotes of his childhood beyond the thin gloss. He doesn't talk about his relationships, deeply anyway, with his master, with Leonard Ho, and with Willie. He'll always say, "Willie is my best friend," but how did they get together? What made them so close? And as soon as I realised that those were the things he didn't talk about publicly often, I knew those were questions I had to ask.

SP: *So was it a process of you drawing him out, rather than that of a big star dictating what he wanted written?*

JY: The thing about Jackie is, he's a director. He's used to being in charge of situations like that. He said to me, that as much as he's made so many things in his life, he's never made a book. He wanted me to know that he saw this not just as him telling the story, but as a collaboration because he's told his story before. He's just never really told this story. It's all Jackie in there, but Jackie is many Jackies. And again, getting behind the very public one, the one everybody knows, is not easy.

I'll be the first to say that there's a lot of stuff not in there that I wish we could have explored more deeply. To the point where even Jackie is aware of this. And he said that he wants me to add another chapter to the mass market paperback edition in which he's really going to—now that he's seen what his fans really want to hear—he's going to really confront the stuff and talk about some of the stuff that even in the book right now is sort of glossed over.

SP: *I've heard the major topics would be the Triads and his personal relationships.*

JY: Those are the two biggest things. His family, his former loves, his son, his wife. In terms of the Triads, obviously some of the incidents were mentioned in the book but there is a reason why Jackie Chan is the one person who has stood up against and does not need to fear the Triads in Hong Kong's film making industry, and that's something that we haven't really sat down and explored.

SP: *Will you have to do more interviews and research or will it be based on what you already know?*

JY: Some of it I already know, but when we started talking about it, I was not informed, per se, but we basically addressed a lot of things that we weren't sure were or were not appropriate to the book. I think initially Jackie said, "I really don't think my fans are curious about that sort of thing." But he's spent weeks on the road now with his fans talking about this book. I think that the questions they've asked lead him to understand that to them, he's more than just what's on screen. So he's given me a little bit more rein to talk more about these things.

Jackie greets the fans at a San Francisco book signing accompanied by bodyguard Ken Low

SP: *Is this addition definite or still in the talking stages ?*

JY: It's definite. It's just a matter of how and when. But it's going to be a pretty significant addition to the book—maybe another 20 or so pages. And it's going to focus on exactly the things that fans asked him about in the course of him promoting this book. It's going to probably be added as an epilogue.

SP: *Under what circumstances did you interview him? Do you speak Cantonese?*

JY: I speak Mandarin. But not so well that I could really communicate a lot of this stuff. So I actually had an assistant, Fon-Lin Nyeu, who handled the translation of idioms. Anytime he couldn't express himself in English appropriately or it was Chinese I couldn't understand, she would step in and make sure we were both clear on what we were talking about. But the reality is, most of the time he was speaking in English. He knew this was going to be first and foremost a gift to his American fans. And because, in a way, his Asian fans and Hong Kong fans know so much about him already, he wanted this book to expressly be something that English speaking fans could really understand. That's part of the reason he decided to do it with a collaborator like me as opposed to doing it in Chinese, let's say with a Chinese speaking journalist and having it translated.

SP: *The text is extremely American in tone. Was this a conscious effort on your part to make it more accessible?*

JY: Not just on my part but on Jackie's and on Peter Borland's and Judith Curr's parts because their feeling was this—as much as Jackie Chan is an international superstar, the one place where he had yet to succeed on the kind of scale he's had elsewhere was America. And I think a lot of the reason why is because in America as much as people admire him, they don't see him as a human being. They see him as a kind of living special effect.

The intent of this book was not only to make it a gift to his American fans, and ultimately to his fans around the world, but really to project him among people in America, people who were just waking up to the idea of who Jackie Chan was, as a real human being who has gone through an unparalleled existence to get where he has today. And essentially I was brought in to bring that perspective to Jackie. The narrative voice is comfortable to Americans because they wanted Americans to read this even if they were not in tune with Hong Kong cinema. Even if they were not aware really of who Jackie Chan was. In talking about the book, in talking about what Jackie Chan's life to date was, they were saying, "This is a guy whose childhood was like a Hong Kong "Angela's Ashes", if not more. This is a human story that goes beyond 'Jackie Chan movie star' and into 'Jackie Chan survivor', in a way." So by translating it that way—and this was done not only with his approval but with his mandate—we hoped that his story could go beyond the ranks of his tried and true hard core fans.

SP: *What does this book offer to people outside this group of hard core fans? It's selling extremely well, and that's more than just his fans.*

JY: That's something that surprised all of us. I don't know to what degree my writing helped. I hope a little bit. It was in the [top 15] best seller list on the New York Times for two weeks running, in the extended list for over a month, it's on the LA Times best seller list and has been there for weeks. It was number one, actually, in the New York Post Barnes and Noble hard cover non-fiction list.

SP: *So to what do you attribute this?*

JY: Part of it is Jackie's tireless promotion. There's nothing that beats having somebody who's willing to walk their book into existence around the world. But after this first meeting I had with Jackie during the reunification, it really came to me that there were global issues and international issues and human issues that were behind Jackie's story. And in framing the book to booksellers, to journalists, there was a real conscious attempt to make Jackie's story a universal story. Something that anybody, even somebody who'd never seen one of Jackie's films, would understand is a monumental story. And Ballantine's done a fantastic job of getting word out about that. I think there's been great word of mouth about the book too.

SP: *The book is structured very much like a film: you have a hero figure who is born into poverty, overcomes great obstacles to reach success, loses his way, finds himself again and emerges at the end a humbler, wiser person for the journey. Was this your intention?*

JY: You are very clever. That's exactly what we thought of when we were structuring this. Like most films these days, there's room for a sequel!

This was me and Jackie first. We had a debriefing session where he gave me an overview of his life, the periods he went through, and I said, "This is a film. Your life's story is as exciting if not more exciting and certainly more dramatic than any film you've actually been in, and most films I've seen on the silver screen." I've seen "Painted Faces", but that only scratched the surface.

So I said, "There are points that we can revolve this around. There's a back story and a thematic resonance to what's going on here. There's a way we can shape this almost as if it were a movie script, with the added advantage that this is a true story." And in talking about these things, the things that were most important to him as well, we realised that the best way to launch the book, literally, was to frame the whole thing as if it were a film.

SP: *It's a flashback sequence.*

JY: Exactly. It's almost classic in a way. You have the face of death, in the face of death you see ghosts, and the ghosts bring you back in time... and he's a child again. If you think about it, the first forty some odd years of the book occur in the three seconds that he's tumbling, which I thought was kind of a funny thing. By being brought back that far, it is a kind of classical structure and most movies are based on classical story structures. You have a hero, and the hero's journey into the underworld in some ways. And in facing death and being changed by that process, as he's forced to face his life to a point where he understands why he has gotten to where he is, that not only allows him redemption but also resurrection. And the final scene where [Jackie] gets up, that's his point of resurrection.

SP: *Did the film format ever effect how you told the story? For example, did you ever leave something out because it didn't fit into the structure?*

JY: What we found was that, remarkably, we had to do little of that. The only thing that was very conscious in terms of restructuring the story to fit that format was the emphasis on the first part of his life in terms of the texture. The reason why we focused on the childhood and early adult stages of his life was because that's all that would fit into this arc right now. By the time he gets to his adulthood, he's at the point of redemption. But I see that the next forty years of Jackie's life are going to be as rich and as full of texture as the first forty, and I believe what this does is it sets him up for people who only know him as this smiling face, this high kicking athlete/actor. So I know that there are people who have said "Why didn't you include his awards [etc]?" The reality is that if we had put it all in one book, the book would have been about 1,000 pages.

SP: *It's true, you don't cover his films, at least the actual making of them.*

JY: It doesn't have much to do with the early part of his life. This is "I Am Jackie Chan" Part One. It's going from young master to a real kind of looking back stage and I think at this point in time, we're reaching him at a kind of apex and there will be a time, I think, when he does a different kind of work. And that work will be one which is probably a lot more reflective, maybe even a lot more textured when it comes to stuff that at this point in his career he's too wrapped up in what he's doing to think about thoroughly. I think he's thought a lot about his childhood and a lot about what's gotten him this far, in terms of things like his adult years, especially the first years in which he really became a superstar. I think there's a lot of stuff that's happened in those years that he still has to confront. So I see it as a multi-stage process.

SP: *Over the years you have become the media anointed spokesman for the Asian American community. Could you elaborate on what Jackie and his success means to the Asian community?*

JY: Jackie has triumphed over incredible challenges in his life as a person, as an individual, and thus is in that way a hero. And he has also triumphed as a person who has gained international recognition in places where you wouldn't even believe people have heard of Asians, much less Jackie Chan—he's a household name. We were in Rotterdam, when he was filming "Who Am I?" and we're walking down the street and little Dutch kids would point him out, and go, "Jackie Chan!" And I'm thinking, "How do they know?" We could just be a bunch of Asian people walking along and yet he's an icon.

But I think, more than that, he is on the leading edge of an internationalisation of cinema which is breaking down some of the most cherished exclusionary principles that have existed in Hollywood. You have for the first time a two-way street happening between Hollywood and the rest of the world. Before, Hollywood exported all its icons to Asia and elsewhere, and continues to do so. But now with Jackie and, after him, Chow Yun Fat, Jet Li, Michelle Yeoh, and others, you finally have the reverse—importing into Hollywood.

> **Jackie has triumphed over incredible challenges in his life as a person, as an individual, and thus is in that way a hero.**

Moreover, for the first time you have an Asian male who against everybody's predictions, against everybody's expectations, has broken through with a blockbuster! I mean, a $100M film, that is the standard, the benchmark. You cannot name another. I mean, Bruce Lee in his day, after his death, when "Enter the Dragon" came out and became an international success, the difference with that was, he was dead! He could not live to both enjoy and build on that success. Since then there has never been an Asian male who has starred in a film that has gotten this kind of success. And the fact that it is Jackie Chan doesn't surprise me but it does encourage me because it means, for the first time, Hollywood and mainstream America has got to realise that heroes come in every colour.

He is Will Smith, you know? I have every belief that just like Will Smith ended up essentially staking his claim as an African American hero, not just to America but to the world, you know Jackie, who has already staked that claim to the world, will stake it to America.

> *Author's Note: The remainder of the interview took place via e-mail. Jeff Yang's replies are presented verbatim, emoticons and all. :)*

SP: *There are some inaccuracies in the book in regards to stunts and accidents. For example, the pole slide stunt in "Police Story" is described as a slide down heavy wires. Will these be corrected in future editions?*

JY: Well, we'll try to make corrections as much as possible (though it looks like we'll be limited in what we can do); the pole-slide/wire thing was a miscommunication (the poles are wrapped with what are essentially Christmas tree lights), due to Jackie's quirky English, and somehow we failed to clarify the situation in the manuscript. There are other errors that either repeat some already-printed misconceptions and/or are the result of Jackie and I not being psychic enough with one another. :)

SP: *Could you shed some light on the Rotterdam stunt, which was used as the framing device? The framing device relies on the imagery of Jackie sliding off the side of the building and falling to the ground below. His resurrection at the end of the book comes when he stands up, surrounded by applauding extras. However, the stunt shown in the film ends before he slides off the side. Was there more to the stunt than they showed? Or were revisions made so the stunt would fit the required imagery?*

JY: There was a certain amount of creative license. However, the stunt was actually done by Jackie and others a number of times in slightly different forms; I was only in Rotterdam for two weeks, and had to write this portion based on what I saw, not on what ended up in the film. I think, as a result, this bit ends up being 'apocryphal' when measured against the final cinematic product—but then again, we don't say that this take was the one that was ultimately used, so...

SP: There are a number of jokes and asides in the appendices, for example a play on the words 'pane' and 'pain'. Are these based on what Jackie said, or are they your own additions?

JY: They are, ahem, my own additions, I guess. Jackie has a swell sense of *verbal* humour that comes out mostly in Chinese; his English doesn't do a good job of translating this, and sometimes his English-language jokes come out seeming like malapropisms (like when he went on David Letterman and was talking about the new 'dress' he bought—to Letterman's amusement). People who see him in English-language interviews tend to think of him as more of a physical comic and a novelty, but he can really tell a story, and he does enjoy the occasional pun. Do Chinese puns translate into English? No. As a result, I tried to give the 'spirit' of his conversational mode, not always the letter. It's a decision that those who actually translate books have to often make, and as a co-author, I had rather more liberty (and mandate to do so) than translators.

SP: Under what circumstances did you interview Jackie? In his office? On the set? What were those sessions like?

JY: In his office, often; on the set, though mostly he was too busy to speak more than conversationally while he was shooting; at dinner in various places, and in a lot of hotel rooms; in the car and other mobile forums. Depending on his level of distraction, these ranged from chaotic to entertaining to immensely enlightening. And occasionally, he'd repeat anecdotes he'd told in different ways at different times, mostly depending on who was listening. :) But I was allowed the freedom to ask him to clarify and expand on anything I was confused by, and Willie helped iron out a lot of things as well.

SP: Some fans who spoke to you on the book tour said you mentioned the possibility of a book being done on Willie Chan. Is this something in the works or something under consideration?

JY: It's a bit of a running joke between us: he certainly has a wonderful story to tell of his own, and one that would probably make a *lot* of important people in Hong Kong and elsewhere angry... if he decided to be as candid about the behind-the-scenes world of HK entertainment as he certainly could be. Most recently, he said to me that even if he did write a book, it could only be published after he retired, or posthumously. :) But if he ever does get around to it, I'll gladly volunteer my humble services... just so I can hear all the gossip!

SP: How has this experience affected your life (if at all) professionally and personally?

JY: It's been very, very interesting. I've learned a lot from Jackie, in addition to learning a lot about him; he's an inspirational and unique individual. Professionally, it was wonderful having the opportunity to work with a star of his calibre, and to help him succeed in the one venue that no one would have thought he might conquer—Jackie (and I) are best-selling authors now! Although I've been getting scads of e-mail suggestions from other people about whom I should co-author books with 'next', as if this were my sole aim in life... though if Michelle Yeoh *did* want me to write a book with her, I don't think I could say no!

I continue to be the publisher of A. Magazine, which is my full-time profession, or more than full-time, really; I intend to write more, though probably a book of my own, rather than a co-written one. Working with Jackie was a singular experience, and one that I don't think I'll ever have the opportunity to supersede...

Until we do volume two, of course! (We'll see!)

Meanwhile, I'm headed to Hong Kong in December, it looks like, to work with Jackie on one last chapter for I AM JACKIE CHAN's paperback edition. It promises to be both revealing and heart-warming—he says he's going to answer a lot of questions that were posed to him during his book tour, including questions about his family, his past romances, and the Triads. And he's going to talk about what it was like, being on the road and interacting with his fans on his book tour and during his super-successful RUSH HOUR experience.

This is exclusive to the paperback, which will come out in June, I believe. So watch out, world: there's still plenty of Jackie left to tell.

STANLEY TONG

The Martial Law Interview!

Screen Power's Renee Witterstaetter interviews Stanley Tong, the man behind the camera for Jackie Chan's 'Supercop', 'Rumble in the Bronx', and 'First Strike', on the Los Angeles set of CBS's new action television series, 'Martial Law'.

Screen Power:

Here we are on the set of 'Martial Law', this time talking to the director of such Jackie Chan movies as 'Supercop' and 'Rumble in the Bronx' as well as 'Mr. Magoo', and now the new television show, 'Martial Law'. Thank you for talking with us. Good to see you again, Stanley.

Stanley Tong:

Thank you. You too.

SP: So, tell us, how did the 'Martial Law' television show come about?

ST: It's actually... it's a long story. When I was 12 years old, I was a big Bruce Lee fan and I loved Bruce Lee movies and that's when I learned martial arts. And since then, I heard an interview where Bruce Lee was saying that he was supposed to be the star of a television show, but he was told that they were not ready to have a Chinese guy to be the star of an American television show. Then, that's why he went back to Hong Kong and did his movies. Once I heard that, actually, I made a wish myself, "I wish I could be an action star, because maybe I can pick up where Bruce Lee left off. Maybe I can do that." The system now, I think about what kind of action show we can do for television. And, I came up here in 1996 and I did 'Mr. Magoo' and I was talking to my producer and I've seen a lot of the computers and TV games and the action is so contemporary—the style and the action is very contemporary. It's very new. And it's taking all these different martial arts from all over the world—Karate, Tai Kwon Do, Kung Fu—you know, everything all together. But when you look at the TV, the action shows are still stuck in the 1980s.

SP: Right.

ST: That style. So, we talked about, "Why don't we come up with a good story and sell it to American television." The President of CBS, he liked the style of what I've done with Jackie Chan: action with comedy and not about violence. So, we had a meeting to talk about the idea and talked about Sammo Hung being a cop from China, who is so big and so fat that no one can believe he can fight, but at the end of the day he gives everyone a big surprise.

And also since he's coming up from China, he has a different background and different training and also has a different way of doing police work. The fish out of water gag that we can play along about the differences between cultures. So it's not just only about martial arts, it's also about different cultures. It can be fresh and have a lot of humour. Les, the CBS President liked the idea very much and he allowed me to have six weeks to draft a show. Before we'd expected to do it mid season, but since Les liked the idea very much we pulled it together within six weeks and shot a half hour presentation which he liked and that's how we got the show.

SP: Is it true that the show was designed for Sammo?

ST: Yeah, yeah. And when we came up with the idea... a lot of people have asked me—I used to have a martial arts school in 1983-84, and when a student came in and asked me, "Well Stanley, what kind of belt do you have?" I told them, "A leather belt." In martial arts you don't have belts. It's like whatever you have, whatever you learn, you don't really need to show off and tell people how good you are. You don't need to look like a martial artist and show off to be cool. It's not the right way to look at martial arts. And Sammo was the perfect person because he doesn't look anything like a martial artist. And that's the good part of it.

SP: But he's so strong. I'm sure it takes a lot of people by surprise when they see him fight.

ST: Yeah.

SP: I was going to say, you started out as a choreographer?

ST: Yes, I started as a stuntman and then became a martial arts choreographer, and then became a director and producer and cameraman and script writer.

SP: And your first jobs were in Hong Kong?

ST: Yes, my first jobs were in Hong Kong in 1980.

SP: And what was that?

ST: I wore wigs and a bra. (laughing)

SP: Oh no, you're kidding? (laughing)

ST: It was a TV show back in 1979. Christmas, I had that job.

Stanley and JC stuntman Mars watch Michelle Yeoh fly on location for 'Police Story 3: Supercop'

SP: We'll have to look up a photo of that (laughing). So, are you doing choreography for 'Martial Law'?

ST: Yeah. And I also brought in my team that used to work with me for a couple of years on the Jackie Chan movies.

SP: Right.

ST: I have the team to help me, and I oversee all the choreography. We have a very good team.

SP: How is working in movies different than working in television?

ST: I think whether you are doing TV or a movie you're doing the same thing, it's one shot at a time. You have to do the same rehearsal. The camera work. The biggest difference is the time. In TV, our show is a seven day show. We have so many first unit days and so many second unit days to pick up all the action. When I directed a Jackie Chan movie, when I choreograph a scene, I can allow two weeks to shoot — 14 days, 13 days. Like in 'Rumble in the Bronx', for one scene I have 14 days of shooting. We have no second unit. First unit shoots everything. And in 'First Strike', when we shoot the last scene — the fight with the ladder — that was 13 days of shooting.

SP: Long time.

ST: In television, we only have one and a half days or two days to shoot a fight scene. It's very tight. What we try to do is, before we shoot, we go and do the choreography on the location. Now we try to get the best out of it. We try to do the choreography before and even try to slip the lighting in on one side. We get a lot in. I find the way we shoot right now is much faster than what I used to do. It's about 40% faster. So later if I do a movie, I don't think I need so much time.

SP: You're next movie will go much faster?

ST: Yeah, yeah. It's also very good because it's a learning process. I never directed TV before and never produced TV before. Now, I'm doing it, I'm learning how to direct a TV show in a limited time and how to work with a schedule, it's a new experience. The show's doing well. I brought in a Hong Kong crew as a second unit to shoot all this action that they are used to doing. They work together very well.

SP: Years ago, Bruce Lee was passed over for 'Kung Fu'. Is this the first appearance of a Chinese lead in an American television show?

ST: Actually the first time an Asian star has been

the lead in a show. You don't really have another show where the star is an Asian on American TV. You might have supporting characters, but you don't have a star like Sammo who is the star of the show. This is the first time. And I can understand the reason. Because we had a meeting at Directors Guild of America several months ago—me, Wing Wayne, Terrance Chang and about 300 Asian filmmakers—to talk about Asian filmmakers in Hollywood, how difficult it is for some of the Asians to get into Hollywood. It's easier for me than for the Asian American directors and filmmakers in the industry. And I guess the reason why they have the problem is because in Hong Kong it's very different. I was in the business 18 years in Hong Kong until now. In Hong Kong we can make four of five movies in a year because of shorter shooting times, so within 18 years I have a lot of experience. I've shot a lot of movies. I did a lot of TV. I did a lot of choreography. So, when I have my resume, it's really long. People can see my experience. But in America, maybe when making a movie it can take years to shoot a movie. So here, to get that experience, it takes a much longer time. Also sometimes when we develop some story idea, most American writers don't understand the culture of the Chinese. And

they don't live there. They weren't brought up there. And it's hard to write a story about a Chinese person week after week and come up with enough stories and have the right understanding of the Chinese culture and how to make the character interesting and believable. How do you make it special and fresh? You really have to have the knowledge of the culture to make a show about that. And also about the action. I'm glad. We're very, very lucky. The show is about Sammo—a cop from China coming to America. He's a Chinese cop, so he can't carry a gun. He's supposed to observe and help. He doesn't have a gun, so every time he bumps into the action he has to use his hands or use any chair or table or ladder as weapons to fight those criminals. That makes him different from all the other cop shows because there's been so much violence using guns. Our style is not out to use a gun. I think that is the difference of what we are bringing the audience. I guess this is why they want to do the show.

SP: *You must be proud to be on such a ground breaking show?*

ST: Yeah. I was very happy about it. And it's a big challenge. It's something I've been longing to do. Now that's happening I'm very happy.

Stanley and JC on the Vancouver set of 'Rumble in the Bronx'

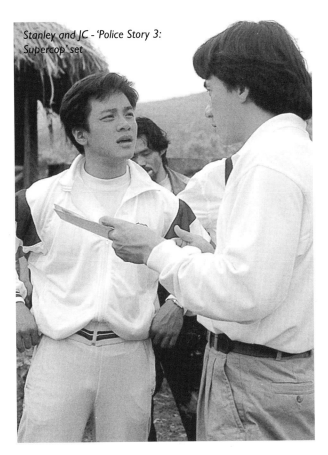

Stanley and JC - 'Police Story 3: Supercop' set

SP: What are the differences between working with Jackie Chan and Sammo Hung?

ST: The difference between working with Jackie and Sammo is there isn't much difference. Because they both have the same background. They both were stuntmen, become action stars, become choreographers, become directors. And, so it's very easy to work with them because the three of us have the same background. So we kind of speak the same language. Whatever... on location if I have to say to Sammo, "This is what I need. I want you to sell this expression a little bit longer." "Because of the cut right?" Or "Move a little." "Because of the lighting right?" "Yeah, okay." When we start the choreography I say, "Let's fight with the chair." He understands and says "Let's do it." If I say, "I want you to have a weapon but not a typical one." "What about a belt?" So he uses a belt as a weapon. Once I tell Sammo the idea, he gets it right away, the same as Jackie. When I say I want to fight with a ladder, we can do this or we can do that. Jackie can already visualise what it's going to be like. So it's much easier to work with guys like Jackie and Sammo as opposed to other actors that don't know about directing, it's much easier. And also they both do choreography. When we start to do a fight they can improvise. That's a plus.

SP: The Western audience is going to be surprised for sure when they see Sammo fight.

ST: Yeah they are going to be. Because he's someone you'd never imagine can do much stuff. It's like the first day, our second producer came on location and watched me shooting the fight. Studio executives were coming over. And Sammo was doing a scene where he was fighting in a shop, standing on a car. Sammo stood up there, someone hit him and he did a back flip and landed on his feet. He did a rehearsal. And the producer was like, "Stanley! Did you see that?" "What? Yeah." "How could he do that? Why don't you get a stunt double for him?" I said, "Well, why are you paying for him? This is what you get!" He can do the stunts on his own. And that's the fun of it. It really surprises everyone what he can do. I think it's because he started martial arts at a very young age. He's not fat then, so he's had all that training until now. He's still practising all those years. He was also working as a choreographer while directing his own movies. So that kept him up in physical fitness.

SP: Will we be seeing any guest stars?

ST: Yeah. Stephen Chow wants to be in it. And Aaron Kwok. We want to bring in some of the very good talent in Hong Kong that a lot of people might not be familiar with. A lot of the great talent in Hong Kong, the Hong Kong movie fans know, but most of this audience does not. But in the near future there won't be any Asian guest stars. It will be mostly an American show to start with. But if we have a good story that fits the part, then we will bring someone in.

SP: I heard that the original idea for 'Martial Law' came from Jackie Chan's 'Supercop'?

ST: Yeah. That's true. When I did 'Supercop' back in 1992.

SP: That's when we met for the first time.

ST: Yes. It was also my first time as a director. I still do remember that. A lot of pressure, but it was very fun. And I liked it.

SP: Yeah, it was.

ST: Then I always feel that if we do something like that—that can work for an American audience, a good story that would make sense of why you have a Chinese cop working in America. If he grows up in America, then he is an American cop. Just because he's Chinese doesn't make any difference. But if he's a cop from China, he has his own country, he has his own way of doing investigation, different ways of training with the martial arts skills. That is something interesting.

SP: *Are you working exclusively in the United States now?*

ST: No, no. Actually for me, coming to America is a learning process. I've been making films for the past 16 years in Hong Kong, and I want to learn different techniques. A different system of making movies. Because in Hong Kong it's more like a family type of system of making movies. But in America it's a very good system that allows me to learn, though some of the ways do waste a lot of money. And in Hong Kong you save a lot of money, but the system is not so good. When you shoot an action type movie, you may not be really able to shoot it because we don't have the system to guide filmmakers to do the work. So, what I try to do is come here and learn a lot more about the American way of film and television and in the future I'd like to go back to Hong Kong and do more interesting Chinese films. That is actually what I really want to do.

SP: *With the Golden Harvest Studios now gone, will it be harder to make films in Hong Kong?*

ST: Not really. Columbia TriStar is establishing a new department in Hong Kong. They want to make Chinese films. High budget, high quality films. People are looking at China—the market will open soon. Even though the economy now is so difficult, in Asia in a couple of years it will come back. It's like a circle all the time in the film industry in Hong Kong. It's up and down. This is good timing to re-organise. To see what is working and what is not working. The filmmakers so often think a lot more when it's the downside and they need to survive, and you tend to think more. When the film industry was very good back in the 80s sometimes there were a lot of movies that didn't make sense. They just came out because of other bad movies. I think I have some faith in Hong Kong movies and Chinese movies. I know directors like John Woo, Ringo Lam, Peter Chan, Tsui Hark, Kurt Wong still want to make good high budget Hong Kong Chinese movies. It's the timing. There are budgets that Hong Kong movies just can't afford. It's so small that it's hard for these directors to go back and do Hong Kong movies. I'm happy that Columbia is taking the first step and trying to produce high profile Hong Kong movies. I'm very happy about that.

Factoids:

Stanley Tong is currently wrapping up production on Shanghai Strike Force, a new action movie being shot in both English and Chinese language versions. The film stars Aaron Kwok Fu-shing, Kenneth Low Wai-kwong, Mark Dacascos and the one and only Won Jin from Operation Scorpio.

Stanley Tong used to be the brother in law of the original Kung Fu movie star, Lo Lieh from Five Fingers of Death, the original breakthrough martial arts movie.

Stanley Tong and Kenneth Low Wai-kwong both doubled the late Brandon Lee during the making of Lee's Hong Kong actioner, Legacy of Rage.

Stanley Tong can be seen in Police Story 3: Supercop as the Mainland Chinese Policeman roughly adjusting Jackie Chan's pose with a few kicks.

Stanley Tong's third movie as director, Project S/Once A Cop or Supercop 2 headlined Michelle Yeoh, and featured a rare cameo appearance by Jackie Chan in drag.

Jackie Chan:
My Stunts

Reviewed by: Lawrence Mak
with Gail Mihara

After much anticipation, the sequel to "Jackie Chan: My Story" has finally hit stores. Whereas in "My Story" Jackie brings fans into his life, in "Jackie Chan: My Stunts" he takes them to work.

A Media Asia film crew followed Jackie for a year to collect the rare footage included in this unprecedented look at the professional life of the world's top action star. But instead of a glossy vanity piece, "My Stunts" plays more like a university film course. Jackie presents a startling amount of practical information that truly gives fans a taste of the work that goes into his seemingly spontaneous moves.

While some press reports have implied that Jackie is revealing his trade secrets in preparation for upcoming retirement, it is clear from the wealth of information contained in this 90 minute documentary that he has more than enough ideas for many more films to come.

Part #1: *Back in the Old Days...*

The documentary opens with a retrospective of the Hong Kong stunt world of the seventies. In addition to showing how things were done back in the "old days", it also pokes fun at how bad some of the techniques were, including the humorous way background stuntmen were used during big fights scenes. (If you've ever watched any Shaw Brothers titles from the seventies, you'll understand.) Jackie himself demonstrates a skilled hand with the classic "blood bag", which he uses to spray the red stuff all over an unfortunate cameraman.

Having set the groundwork for the rest of the programme, Jackie discusses how he improved on those methods when choreographing fight scenes with multiple opponents. Here the fan sequence from "Young Master" makes a welcome return during a discussion of how Jackie adapts traditional kung fu for the screen. He also takes the camera into the gym so fans can see how certain basic flips, jumps and rolls are carefully integrated into seemingly spontaneous fight scenes.

Next Jackie re-visits some familiar places and stunts from his movies, with an emphasis on "Police Story 1"—the umbrella stunt, the slope run, and the legendary Wing-On Plaza bust-up at the end of the movie. At each location he discusses how he planned the stunts, what was going through his mind when he performed them and how dangerous they were. You never realise how steep that slope is until you see it from Jackie's point of view. (Very scary...)

Part #2: *The Stunt Lab*

The next section features the "stunt lab", where Jackie stores some of his memorabilia. It is also a place for testing out ideas he devises "while in the shower and driving."

This is a very interesting and fun section, as you'll shake your head in disbelief at how Jackie and his boys perform seemingly simple, yet effective tricks. You'll also discover that no matter how well planned their fight sequences are, it requires numerous takes to get everything right.

This section should be re-titled "A Tribute to the Jackie Chan Stunt Team", as fans are finally able to see them on camera clearly, without blurs. Jackie's boys showcase their formidable talents in a mock race to grab a package hanging from the rafters. While they perform the usual fights and falls one would expect, some of the stunts the younger members pull off are truly horrific and very impressive.

Part #3: *The Prop Room*

After an interlude covering explosives and the use of fire arms, Jackie discusses the importance of "utilising your surroundings." With help from his stunt team, Jackie casually crafts intricate fight sequences using everyday objects, including fridges, trolleys, lamps, chairs, tables, record sleeves(!) and the infamous ladders (both bamboo and aluminium).

Anyone interested in making his or her own action film should certainly study this last section. In a surprisingly in-depth sequence, his stunt team and students perform several perfectly executed action sequences. Afterwards the outtakes show just how long it took to get the final product. Jackie himself dissects each take with merciless perfectionism and identifies what's wrong, why one take works and another doesn't, and ways to do seemingly dangerous stunts safely.

But lest some of his more impressionable viewers think that falling from a second story level onto the roof of a car is "do-able", Jackie constantly stresses, "don't do this at home; they are all VERY dangerous."

Illustrating how Jackie puts his theories into practise, the documentary also takes fans into the field. Behind-the-scenes footage from "Who Am I?" shows Jackie prowling the rooftop location in search of inspiration.

Perusing an air vent as well as the steep drop from the roof's edge, Jackie begins to craft possible scenarios for the coming fight sequence. Footage of Jackie working with high-kicker Ron Smoorenburg also illustrates how difficult and specialised the "Jackie" style of movie fighting is, as Ron struggles to learn the special "rhythm" in fight scenes that Jackie single-handedly pioneered.

"Jackie Chan: My Stunts" is available in both English and Mandarin (with English subtitles). To preserve authenticity, each scene involving narration or explanation by Jackie was filmed twice—once in Mandarin and once in English. Since Jackie is (naturally) more expressive in Mandarin, the Mandarin version contains three more minutes of information. Therefore, we suggest that English-speaking viewers first watch the English version to understand what each scene is about, then experience the subtitled Mandarin version to glean a bit more wisdom from The Master.

Though three minutes shorter, the English version has an extra section not available on the Mandarin. Entitled "Idea Wall", this section features Jackie and his vast library of information, to be used when coming up with stunt ideas.

The visual aspect of the documentary is above average, at the same level as "My Story". The real improvements come with the other technical touches. The visual graphics and computer generated images are used sparingly and effectively. The subtitles are much improved as well, with only the occasional typographical or grammatical error as opposed to "My Story", where every subtitle contained a mistake

All in all, this is one Jackie video that every Chan fan should possess, no matter which era of his works you are interested in.

Secrets Revealed:

"Police Story" Bus Stunt: Instead of using a regular umbrella, Jackie had one constructed of iron to support his weight. The rest was just good upper body strength.

"Police Story" Run Down the Hillside: No tricks here. This is pure Jackie but the actual incline of the hillside used is revealed and it looks even scarier on video than it does in the film.

Kick in the Face: Do not try this at home. Instead of using a regular shoe to connect with the face for a close-up, Jackie uses specially constructed "Power Shoes" that inflict only 1/10th of the impact. Coupled with a light kick and good opponent reaction, the blow seems real indeed. A sprinkle of dust on the shoe to disperse on contact completes the effect.

DVD INFO

First the format. This DVD contains both the Mandarin and English versions, has 8 language subtitles, Dolby Digital 5.1, plays anywhere except Japan (regions 1-5) and is copy-protected with Macrovision. However there is a bit of misleading info: while it says the documentary is in letterbox format, only film footage in the documentary is letterboxed; the documentary itself is in fullscreen.

The discs also contain two trailers for the documentary, a 2 minute short version and a 13 minute complete version.

JC performs a stunt in 'My Stunts'

Golden Harvest
presents

GORGEOUS

Starring

Jackie Chan. Shu Qi. Tony Leung Chiu-wai. Emil Chau Wah-kin.

Bradley James Allan. Kenneth Low Wai-kwong. Kwan Yeung.

Cameo appearances by

Dan Wu. Stephen Fung. Ken Wong. Sandra Ng. Sam Lee.

Annie Wu. Eric Kok. Vincent Gok. Tony Oi-lin. And Stephen Chiau Sing-chi.

Directed by

Vincent Gok.

Action Choreography

Jackie Chan. Jackie Chan Stuntmen's Club. Frankie Chan.

Reviewed by Mike Leeder

'Gorgeous' (Chinese title: 'The Glass Bottle') is not exactly the kind of title that you associate with a Jackie Chan movie, is it? But then again, this is a very different Jackie Chan movie. For a start it marks the end of an era as the last film to be shot at the Golden Harvest Studios in Diamond Hill, and secondly it's a romantic comedy, a love story!

The film opens in a Taiwanese village where beautiful young Bu (Shu Qi) seeks true love as demonstrated by her parents, her Hong Kongese mother Elaine Kam and Taiwanese father Chan Chung-yung. One day she finds a romantic message in a bottle, "I'm waiting for you. Love Albert!" and despite the protests of her would be boyfriend Longy (Cheng Chun-gai), she takes flight to Hong Kong, sure that Albert is the man of her dreams.

Upon her arrival in Hong Kong, she soon finds Albert (Tong Leung), and while it is true that he too seeks true love, unfortunately for her it is also of the male variety. But life goes on and so does the plot, Ah Bu manages to save Hong Kong businessman and playboy CN Chan (Jackie Chan) from the clutches of his rival in business LW (Emil Chau). While CN is charmed by Bu's beauty, she decides to try and hook CN by hook or by crook. Throw in a case of mistaken identity between Bu and the girlfriend of a Taiwanese mobster, Longy coming to Hong Kong in search of Bu, and LW's plan to discredit CN Chan by having him beaten by a western martial arts fighter (Brad Allan), and you pretty much have the plot for this film.

Now while a lot of people (you know who you are!) have been very quick to dismiss this film as a Jackie Chan pot-boiler rushed out for Chinese New Year, and I do have to say that when I visited the set during production at the invitation of my old buddy Frankie Chan who was lending a hand with action directing chores, and Jackie and Frankie admitted that they didn't have as much time to spend on the movie as they wanted, even I began to wonder... It is a fun movie. I enjoyed it a lot more than some of Jackie's movies in the past. It's not the greatest Jackie Chan movie ever made, but it's still more enjoyable than 'First Strike' and 'City Hunter' in my opinion! What you have to remember is that it's not a slam bang in your face non stop Jackie Chan action movie, it's a lighter paced romantic comedy with four crisply choreographed Jackie Chan fight scenes, a great training montage and a lot of humour.

The plot is a bit ropey and the relationship between Jackie and Shu Qi doesn't have as much chemistry as it should have some of the time, but it's a lot of fun. Jackie gets to play with his supposed real life playboy image in his reel life role as CN Chan, and seems to be having fun doing it. And physically he's still the man, he's punching, kicking, flipping and diving to full effect and shows off some nice Wing Chun handwork again for the first time since 'Rumble in the Bronx' during his training montage. And the man can still move, the first two fight scenes in the film are merely a warm up for his two bouts with Brad Allan who gives Jackie his toughest test since Ken Low in 'Drunken Master 2', and when these two go one on one, it's worth every penny.

Taiwanese beauty Shi Qi plays the role of Bu with her normal naive charm, and continues to prove that she's one of the best actresses in Hong Kong cinema in every project. Throw in the fact that she's far too cute and has got the most appealing voice and physicality and where can you go wrong. Tong Leung Chiu-wai lets loose in his first non-dramatic role in a long time, and camps it up bigtime as Bu's big sister Albert, mincing around the film like Richard Simmons in a role done as a debt of gratitude to the late Leonard Ho of Golden Harvest. His performance is far from politically correct but it's fun, as is the whole movie. Singer Emil Chau finally gets to do more than sell ice-cream ('Rumble in the Bronx' and 'Mr. Nice Guy') or help with the theme song ('Who Am I?') in a Jackie Chan movie this time, and plays the self-obsessed LW with a certain amount of charm. Singer Chan Chung-gai does the best he can with his underdeveloped role as Jackie's would be rival in love, while veteran Taiwanese actor Chan Chung-yung (Jet Li's father in law in 'Fong Sai-yuk') proves his broad comedic skills are still as sharp as his voice is loud.

As for the cameos, while Dan Wu, Stephen Fung, Ken Wong, Eric Kok, Vincent Gok, Sam Lee, Tong Oi-lin and a blink and you'll miss her Annie Wu are fun for star spotters, Sandra Ng gets to mistake Chan Chung-gai for Chow Yun-fat while Stephen Chiau Sing-chi turns up in the largest cameo as a harassed Hong Kong Police Dog Handler, with Jackie repaying the favour by turning up very briefly in Stephen Chiau's Chinese New Year release 'King of Comedy'. Jackie's long-time bodyguard, friend and Screen Power interviewee Kenneth Low might not get to do much fighting this time, throwing only a few moves in the film's first two action sequences, but he does get to show his comedic skills to good effect in the film (he also boasts a very nice lack of hair—much like my own!). Kwan Yeung, last seen as Jackie's Chinese adversary in the finale of 'Who Am I?', and long-time friend Ah Tuen crop up throughout the film, while the real discovery of the film is the aforementioned Brad Allan.

Brad is an Australian martial artist/stuntman who has worked with Jackie since 'Mr. Nice Guy'. He'd done background stunts in the last few films before Jackie invited him to step up to bat for 'Gorgeous', and the boy's done good! Brad is a lifelong Jackie Chan fan, highly talented martial artist and gymnast, and a hell of a nice guy to boot. I had the opportunity to hang out with him during his stay in Hong Kong for the film, and an exclusive interview with him shall soon be forthcoming in everybody's favourite magazine. Brad plays Alan, a fighter brought in to

JC and 'Gorgeous' co-star, Shu Qi - Golden Harvest Studios car park

fight and humiliate Jackie by his rival. And in their first fight that's exactly what he does, displaying a varied amount of crisp martial arts styles and boxing against Jackie. But it's more a gentlemanly fight than a big brawl, both wear gloves and neither tries to kill the other, and the change in idea works well. The first fight was filmed in freezing conditions atop the carpark in Ocean Terminal, Tsim Sha Tsui, over a couple of cold wet nights, and he does the business. And for the finale where he and Jackie have their rematch after Jackie's gone off and 'Rocky'd up for the second bout, it's tough fighting, with the two of them trading punches, kicks, jump kicks and much more to full effect in a lengthy bout that pays off the rivalry between them in the film without it becoming a deathmatch. And for his first real acting role of any kind, Brad not only proves he can move, but he also comes across as an actor. His performance definitely shows a lot of promise, and I wish him all the best with his future plans and intentions of continuing his work for Jackie. I'd also like to go on record as stating that Brad Allan is, without any question, the only western martial artist to be considered as a member of Jackie Chan's stunt-team, and that's according to Mr. Chan himself! (Brad also turns up performing a fight scene in the new 'Jackie Chan: My Stunts' documentary.)

Now as I've said, try and see this movie with an open mind. It's exactly what it was intended to be, a fun movie and it's got some great action. Jackie's boatbound action scene against Ken Low, Kwan Yeung and the boys. Jackie's premiere demonstration of motorcycle fu as he takes on and out several masked baseball bat wielding attackers through the use of a motorcycle and his opponents' weapons! The two fight scenes with Brad Allan that I'm sure a lot of people will be adding to their list of top ten fight scenes. A great training montage with Jackie doing weights, skipping, Wing Chun, some evil boxing. What else has it got? Some good humour, a lot of fun cameos, Annie Wu (Haaaa!), Shu Qi! And of course Jackie Chan. What more could you want! It's nice to see a slightly more light hearted Jackie again. Yeah I still want to see Jackie doing more, and bigger, action films, but this is a pleasant reminder of some of Jackie's older, less serious projects, so check it out!

CITY HUNTER

Explored!

Richard Cooper explores "City Hunter", Jackie Chan's 1992 action comedy manga-movie.

Manga has been very well known in Japan for many years - but has only become popular in the West over the last few years . The English-dubbed video release of "City Hunter" was surprisingly well timed (not to mention lucky) in the West, because the video was brought out during the boom of both Manga comics and videos which were starting to frequent the stores over here. The video release also coincided nicely with the ever so popular arcade beat-em-up, "Street Fighter 2".

For those of you who haven't watched "City Hunter" before, and would like to know why Japanese comics and an arcade game are associated with this Jackie Chan movie, well, for a start

Jackie's character in the film is based on a very popular Japanese comic book character called Ryu Saeba (or Mambo) and regarding the "Street Fighter 2" game (which I for one put a lot of money into during my teen-years!) well, during one of the end fight scenes, Jackie transforms into two of the game's characters.

Jackie is joined by two of Japan's most popular actresses for this movie, Kumiko Goto and Joey Wong, and all characters work well together here. Hong Kong film buffs usually see Joey Wong flying around in the "Chinese Ghost Story" films, but they should be pleasantly surprised to see Wong with her feet firmly on the ground this time around.

Behind-the-scenes of 'City Hunter'

Actor Michael Wong pops up in the first couple of scenes before dying off. Fans wanting to see more of him (on screen that is!) can check out his hardcore cop character in "Thunderbolt".

Briefly, the story revolves around Ryu Saeba, a well known Hong Kong womanising private investigator! Yeah, doesn't sound like one of Jackie's usual characters does it? Still it's just a movie, and that's what's important to remember. Anyway, Jackie's character is asked to find a rich Japanese man's runaway daughter (who is played by Kumiko Goto). Joey Wong plays his faithful assistant, who also very much wants to be his girlfriend, and most times makes a lot of hints

> **Fight-fans won't be disappointed here, as Jackie and his stunt team choreograph some excellent scenes. Admirers of the 70s kung fu flicks will especially enjoy seeing Jackie fighting with a few traditional weapons in the 90s.**

concerning the subject - but Jackie stays quite oblivious to this.

Ryu Saeba agrees to take on the job and looks around Hong Kong for the girl, and after being chased by a gang of school kids on skateboards he eventually follows Kumiko on board of a luxury cruise, where Joey Wong is also on board with her cousin trying to make Jackie jealous!!! And it doesn't end there, to this already complicated but very funny storyline add in veteran Hong Kong villain Richard Norton and his gang of thugs who plan to take over the cruise and rob everyone, and you have "City Hunter".

In the end the hero is there to reunite the father and daughter, and also manages to save the ship in the process - all in a day's work for Jackie Chan.

Fight-fans won't be disappointed here, as Jackie and his stunt team choreograph some excellent scenes. Admirers of the 70s kung fu flicks will

especially enjoy seeing Jackie fighting with a few traditional weapons in the 90s.

My only criticism of the movie overall was that Wong Jing directed it! Jackie, who was only in charge of the action, as usual didn't disappoint, but with a director like Wong Jing whose humour is a little strange - no, I'm being too polite here, his humour is downright weird!!! - it does downplay the movie a little... So it's safe to assume that Jackie and Wong Jing do not complement each other in a film. Overall though, it's still got some great action and of course our man Chan, so it's not that bad.

Lastly, for those of you who do not know what Manga is, well (and I hope I don't offend any Manga fans out there because this is only my opinion!) it's a well drawn, and often futuristic detailed cartoon-movie with a lot of sex and violence - but we won't go there! Also worth mentioning, "Hong Kong Cat 3" star Chingamy Yau also starred in the film, no doubt due to Wong Jing's power and influence - but we won't go there either!

Brad Allan

An Australian Stuntman in King Jackie's Court

By
Mike Leeder

"Always Two There Are, a Master and His Apprentice!"

"Always Two There Are, a Master and His Apprentice!" So spoke no less an authority than Yoda in George Lucas's The Phantom Menace, and few if any would doubt that without question Jackie Chan is the Master of action movies. For more than twenty years he has ruled the Asian box office, and a few short years ago he started making inroads into the American/International market with the success of Rumble in the Bronx. And in the summer of 1998 he consolidated his success when his team up with Chris Tucker and New Line Cinema for Rush Hour broke box office records worldwide.

Many a western martial artist has dreamed of working with Jackie Chan, including myself, and while some lucky ones have worked with Jackie in his movies, despite what you may have heard somewhere or may have been told - no westerner has ever been a member of the Jackie Chan Stuntmen's Club/Sing Gaban. Possession of a Jackie Chan Stuntmen's Club T-shirt despite their value, doesn't make you a member. I've got a shirt, and I've worked on more than a few movies since I came to Hong Kong but that doesn't make me a member. I repeat, no western martial artist/stuntman has ever become a member of Jackie's action team - until now that is! The man who has achieved the seemingly impossible by being taken on by Jackie as his apprentice is Brad Allan. Brad is a soft-spoken Australian martial artist who first worked with Jackie on Mr. Nice Guy and has worked with Jackie on every project since. Not to mention being given the opportunity of a lifetime - to go one on one with Jackie in his most recent Hong Kong release, Gorgeous, which by the time you read this will have just premiered in the US. Brad goes toe to toe with the man himself.

I caught up with Brad for the following interview.

Mike Leeder:

Brad, can I start off by asking you for some biographical details, where were you born and raised?

Brad Allan:

I was born and raised in Melbourne, Australia.

ML: How and why did you first get involved with the martial arts?

BA: It was when I was about ten years old, I was small for my age and got pushed around quite a bit. So my father took me to the local Karate school where I began my martial arts studies in Goju-kai Karate.

ML: How far did you take your Karate studies before moving on to other martial arts?

BA: I must have studied Karate for about four years. By that time I had started watching Jackie Chan films and it was pretty obvious that what he did wasn't Karate, it was something else. So I began looking around for another martial art, and at the same time I began to dabble with gymnastics. But I do have to say that regarding martial arts and so much more, Jackie Chan has been my biggest influence. I looked at what Jackie can do, and knew that I wanted to be able to do some of the stuff that he could do. I saw him flip and realized that I should start learning gymnastics if I wanted to do anything like he did. And when I discovered Wushu, which was the closest style I could find to anything that Jackie was doing in his films, I got right into that.

ML: Did you begin your Wushu studies under the Chinese National Champion - Liang Chang-Xing?

BA: Yes. After leaving Karate, I had begun to study Wing Chun at William Cheung's school. One day as I was leaving the class I saw this small Chinese guy moving and kicking like you wouldn't believe. And I knew that I wanted to learn what he was doing, so I went over and introduced myself to him, and he was indeed Liang Chang-Xing. (Liang Chang-Xing was Jet Li's teammate on the Beijing Wushu Team and Xing-Yi Champion of China for several years.)

Chang-Xing said that he would take me as his first student in Melbourne (Australia), but William Cheung said that I couldn't train with

Chang-Xing unless I brought in 7 or 8 people and we had a legitimate class. William Cheung had brought Chang-Xing over to Australia to teach Tai-Ji, and I don't think he was very happy about him teaching Wushu on his own. So I got about 10 friends together and we started studying Wushu with Chang-Xing. I spent about five years with Chang-Xing before I went on to university. I was studying Asian culture, politics, history etc and Mandarin Chinese. And I was offered a scholarship to continue my Chinese language studies over in Shanghai and I jumped at the chance.

ML: *Did you continue with your martial arts studies in China?*

BA: While my initial reason for going to China was to study the language, I did want to continue my martial arts studies, and I went on to live and study Wushu at the Shanghai Sports Institute. I was studying there on and off for about a year and a half including some time in Beijing.

ML: *It was while you were in China that you made your first film appearance in Liu Chia-Liang's ill fated Drunken Master 3.*

BA: You know too much! (laughing) At that time whenever movie companies filming in Shanghai wanted any western martial artists or extras for a film, they would come down to the foreign dormitory at the University and hire people for their films. And I got asked if I would like to work on Drunken Master 3, and I thought why not. I would like to make it clear that I'm not the main western villain in the film, that was some Italian Wushu guy, I was pretty much just an extra in the film. It was by no means a great movie, but it was fun and I did enjoy the experience of working on a film.

ML: *Had you always been interested in getting involved in the film industry, or had you just enjoyed the films and the martial arts without really thinking of any crossover between the two?*

BA: As I've mentioned, Jackie has always been a very big influence on me martial arts and otherwise, and yes I was very interested in working in films, but I never really had any idea of how to do it. That's one of the reasons why I went to University, I thought I'd complete my education and then see what direction my

The finale of 'Gorgeous'

The final showdown: Brad vs JC

life was headed in. I've never really thought of myself as an actor of any kind. I thought I might be able to be a stuntman if I was lucky and got to work with the right people. I've long been a fan of Jackie's work, and he has been by far the biggest influence on me in the martial arts path I've followed, the philosophies I've embraced, the interest in Chinese culture etc. I've always loved movies and would have taken any chance to get into films but I just didn't really know how to do it at the time.

When I worked on Drunken Master 3, I became acquainted with the Shanghai based action/stunt co-ordinator. I showed him some video footage that myself and Chang-Xing had shot, we'd both played around with ideas of how to shoot martial arts for film before, and he seemed quite interested in me and actually invited me to stay in Shanghai, and sign a contract to join his stunt team. Although for various reasons I turned down his offer, I did have some regrets about not staying on to do films, but things seem to have turned out OK since then.

ML: *It must have been quite soon after your return to Australia that you got involved with the proposed film project with Liang Chang-Xing and my mentor and longtime friend Hong Kong action director Alip Sak.*

BA: I came back from Shanghai, and graduated. I was still training in Wushu, but Chang-Xing had moved on to live and train with members of a religious group in Queensland (Australia). So I continued my studies under Tang Lai-Wei who had also been on the Beijing Wushu team with Jet Li and Chang-Xing. I have been very fortunate to have had some world-class Wushu athletes as my coaches. The combination of their attitudes and training mentality has had a huge impact on my life.

Chang-Xing called me up and told me that the group he was working for were looking at doing some action film and television projects and had some guys from Hong Kong and Taiwan coming to help them, and it might be a good chance for me to learn from them and help out. So I went up to Queensland to join them for a while.

When I got there I met up with Alip, who is a very good choreographer and action director, and a couple of stunt-guys he'd brought in from Taiwan. They all blew me away with what they could do, and one of the Taiwanese stuntmen really impressed me with his acrobatic abilities. I only stayed with them for a few weeks, during which time I learnt quite a bit and realized that movie fighting was a very different martial art to anything else I'd ever studied.

ML: Did the few weeks working with Alip and his stunt-guys have much of an effect on you?

BA: It changed my whole concept of martial arts, it made me rethink the way I trained, the way I did things, and made me realize that I had so much more I needed to work on. I thought that these guys represented all Asian stuntmen, and that if I ever wanted to work with them, I had to try and be as good as they were if I wanted a chance. So I started training harder than ever, six hours a day, very intensively. I got very heavily into gymnastics again from this point. It wasn't so much that these guys could do high falls and reactions, it was the range of their abilities. One of the Taiwanese guys especially impressed me: if he wanted to impress someone who was watching, he would do X amount of flips or some physical action that you might not really need to do in a movie, he'd go overboard. And that impressed me. I realized that being able to take a hit, or pull off a good reaction wasn't enough. I needed to have that extra special something to get me through the door, to give me a chance to do the job. I knew that I needed a bigger variety of moves.

I went back to watching Jackie's movies, but with a better eye for what he could do. It became really clear to me, Jackie can dance, he can kick, he can tumble, he can box, and he can pretty much do it all. For movies you can't really be just one style, you've got to be diverse. I got into dancing, gymnastics, boxing, Aikido; I studied a bit of everything, anything that would give me further skills to use for films.

I am not really a gymnast, but at least I can do a double back, which is a level 10 gymnastic move. I can do a double back which is a decent move for a gymnast. I can do a tornado kick and land in the splits, which is a

pretty decent move for a Wushu player. I can do a good number of decent moves in a number of different things. I'm not saying I'm really good at anything, I'm not. What I do have is a pretty big varied bag of tricks that I can use to let people believe I'm quite good at what I do, and that has been one of my aims. I deal in illusion. I'm not the greatest gymnast or the greatest kicker, but I can make you believe that I am pretty good at what I'm doing.

ML: You can definitely flip and fly, having seen you in action on film, your showreel and in the flesh, do you have proper gymnastic qualifications?

BA: No, I've just worked at it. My friend Debbie Inkster is a gymnastics instructor, her brother Darin is an Olympic level gymnast now working with the Cirque du Soleil and I've spent a lot of time working with both of them. Yes, I've worked at my gymnastics but I haven't worked my way through the system of levels that gymnasts have to work through. I've dabbled but I'm not really a gymnast as such. It's the same with tumbling, I've just

Brad the Indian Warrior! On location for 'Shanghai Noon'

recently gotten into tumbling, and that's another skill that I'm going to work at. I've studied a lot of different styles, many of them purely to give me that edge, a wider variety of movements I can bring to a film.

ML: *After you came back from China and your experience with Alip and Chang-Xing, had you tried to get involved with the Australian stunt industry?*

BA: In Melbourne where I live, there's really only one stunt group and they're called New Generation Stunts. They pretty much have the monopoly for stunts in my area, and they do quite a lot of work. I did go and audition for them and they seemed to like what I could do, because they offered me a position with them. Unfortunately for me, the projects that they have been involved in haven't had much use for my abilities. In fact it is typical of most stunt teams in western countries, they are often well trained in high falls, car stunts, fire stunts, etc. Their fight choreography, in my opinion, is outdated and boring. With Jackie's films and others like The Matrix, audiences are discovering quality film fighting that is new and exciting and Hollywood is having to hire Hong Kong action directors because their western counterparts still have no idea how to design this kind of action.

ML: *I know you did a student film with a rather memorable name around this time...*

BA: Yeah, a film called Deep Shit! This was a project for a student at the VCA (Victoria College of the Arts). His name is Morgan Evans; he was another student of Chang-Xing's and was studying with me when I was teaching Wushu at Melbourne University. He came up with the concept and put together the project and asked me to get involved, which I did.

The film did well for Morgan; he got a lot of good reactions and exposure from the project, while I'm not 100% satisfied with the action we did for the film. I did get to do a few things that I had been wanting to try out on film. Some of the stunts and fight scenes are OK, they show that there is some potential for the people involved. For what it is, it's not too bad. I choreographed my action scenes while Morgan did the stuff he was in.

ML: *Did you work on any other projects before*

you got involved with Jackie Chan on the Mr. Nice Guy/Superchef! film?

BA: No, I was preparing to compete in Wushu at the time, but as soon as I found out that Jackie was in town, because he's always been such an idol of mine, I really wanted to get a chance to see him, even if I couldn't work with him. I called up New Generation and asked them if it would be possible for me to get on the set even if it was just as an observer. They agreed and I went down to the set and met with the Australian stunt co-ordinator. They were about 4 months into filming the movie, so I didn't think I'd have any chance of working on the film, but I was happy just to be an observer. But as it happened, they were having a lot of problems with local guys not being able to catch the Hong Kong choreographic style.

I came to the set straight from teaching a Wushu class. I had with me a letter of recommendation in Chinese that Chang-Xing had given me previously when I'd gone to China, and when I met with the film's Hong Kong action director Cho Wing (superkicker extraodinaire from Bury Me High and Nocturnal Demon, and student of the one and only Tsui Siu-Ming), I gave it to him. He asked me about my martial arts background and asked me to show him what I could do. I ran through a variety of moves and I guess he liked what I could do, because he hired me to work on the film.

ML: *How did you feel to finally meet Jackie Chan, and then get the chance to work with him?*

BA: I went up to him on the set, and introduced myself to him, we started talking, and I think that the fact I could speak Mandarin surprised him. He was very warm and friendly, and I was surprised at just how solid he is in person, Jackie is a big guy when you meet him. It was the best day of my life, just getting the chance to meet my hero blew me away and then it got even better when they asked me to come back and work with him. It was without a doubt a dream come true.

I came back and started filming the next day. I think Jackie and his team liked the fact that I could catch his tempo and rhythm a bit better than some of the other guys. I remember at one point he said to one of his stunt team, Man Ching, that they should bring myself and another Australian martial artist working on the film, Paul Andreovski, back to Hong Kong for more work. I wasn't sure if he was joking or not, but it was very exciting to hear him say it anyway.

ML: *How long did you work on the film for?*

BA: I was on the film for about a month and a half. We shot the big fight scene in the construction site and then went on to Sydney for the finale. I really enjoyed working with Jackie and his team, all of the stunt team were very helpful, and made me feel comfortable working with them.

ML: *How about the intricacies of Jackie's choreography? Did you find it easy to get the hang of Hong Kong action?*

BA: It was difficult to begin with. When I'd tried to imitate Hong Kong action on viceo before, if we performed at normal speed, it seemed too slow, so we had worked on speed and performed it as fast as we could to get that Hong Kong style. I didn't know about frames per second, and how film can make you look faster while video slows you down. So it was frustrating in the beginning, because whenever I did a combination at Jackie, I'd be going at a hundred miles an hour because that was how I'd been training. I had to learn how to slow down, how to break down a fight scene, to get used to the tempo of a fight. It's something that I still have a problem with even today.

But Jackie and his team were very good about everything; yes I made some mistakes, but I think they could all see just how much I was into what I was doing, and how eager I was to learn everything that I could. I wanted to know about the camera angles, the lenses they were using, the frames per second, everything. The fact that I didn't just look at it as a job, I looked at it the way I still do, it's a learning experience, it helped me.

ML: *After the film wrapped, did you think there would be any further opportunities to work with Jackie?*

BA: At the wrap party, I went up to Jackie and thanked him for giving me this opportunity and for making my dream come true. Jackie said,

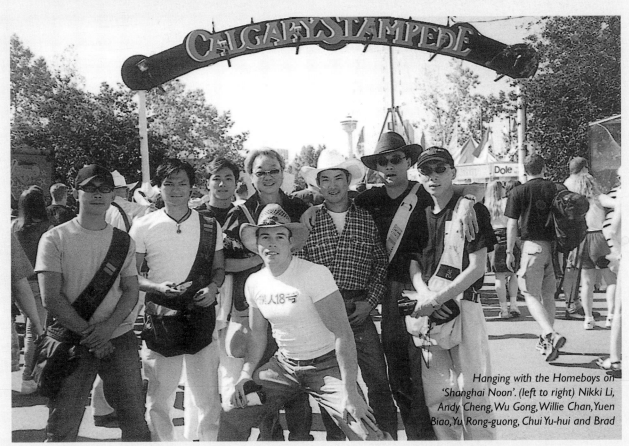

Hanging with the Homeboys on 'Shanghai Noon'. (left to right) Nikki Li, Andy Cheng, Wu Gong, Willie Chan, Yuen Biao, Yu Rong-guong, Chui Yu-hui and Brad

"Don't worry, I'll call you for the next film." I wasn't too sure if he was serious, but it did give me some hope, and sure enough a few months later Paul and myself both got a call asking us if we were available to work on Who Am I? Everything Jackie has ever said to me, he has delivered on. He has always been true to his word to me.

ML: On Who Am I? what were you doing? Was it background stunts, doubling, choreography?

BA: I think it was Jackie's idea, he took Paul and myself (who plays the lime green suited bad guy in the clog fight in Holland) under his wing. He wanted us to learn everything we could; we lived and worked with Jackie's stunt team for the movie. We learnt about doubling, reactions, choreography, rigging stunts, everything. It wasn't that we were hired to act in the film, although Paul did play a small role in the end, it was that Jackie wanted us to learn how they did everything.

We worked on the film on and off for the whole shoot. We went to South Africa for a couple of months then we went on to work in Holland for the finale and Malaysia for the opening. It was such a big film and they shot so much that wasn't used, it could easily have been a three hour movie or two two hour movies, Who Am I? parts 1 and 2.

ML: You did a variety of doubling work in the film, including several sections of the end fight when Jackie takes on stuntman Kwan Yeung and Dutch kicker Ron Smoorenburg. It's funny considering how much press Mr. Smoorenburg got himself and the numerous claims he made about his ability and work on the film, that he is doubled so many times by yourself, and several other members of the Jackie Chan stunt team, as is shown in Media Asia's Jackie Chan: My Stunts.

BA: They had a lot of problems with this guy. There is no doubt that Ron is a very good kicker. But he just couldn't get the tempo of film fighting; he couldn't get his timing or the combinations down properly. Jackie was very patient with him but despite so many attempts he couldn't get the hang of the action properly. One day, he was meant to do a kicking combination and I was trying to work with him to show him how to get the moves down. I

was going through the combination, and Jackie saw me do it, and told me to put on his costume and do the moves for him. Myself, Jackie's number two Nicky Li, Sam Wong, and Andy Cheng (also Sammo Hung's stunt double on Martial Law) all doubled for him at various points in the fight. I doubled a number of people in the film.

ML: What came after Who Am I? Did you have a contract with Jackie for the next film?

BA: It's funny but apart from for the most recent film, Gorgeous/The Glass Bottle, I've never really had a printed contract. It's been a personal contract from me to Jackie. I will always commit myself and make myself available to Jackie. He has been such a great influence on me, and has given me so many opportunities that I will always be there if he needs me.

ML: After Who Am I? what were you doing?

BA: I was working in the Australian stunt industry, and while a few things came along, it wasn't really enough to earn a living from. I did some stunt related courses, taught Wushu and worked in a library to earn my living. I was preparing to enter international Wushu competition and there was always the possibility of another movie with Jackie, but nothing was definite. So I was still training very hard because I didn't want an opportunity to come along and I wouldn't be ready for it.

I thought it might be an idea to come to Hong Kong and see if anything was happening, and if nothing was happening, I'd go onto China and prepare for competition. While I was in Hong Kong Nicky was preparing to go to Philadelphia to do the choreography for a video for the Wu Tang Clan, and he asked me to go with him.

ML: You also turned up in Media Asia's Jackie Chan: My Stunts documentary around this time. You not only perform background stunts, but are also given a nice fight scene showcasing your talent as a performer along with Jackie's choreographic skills.

BA: Nicky was heavily involved in this program, and he's a very good friend and has taken care of me since I've known him. He asked me to help him on this project and while at first I wasn't really doing much on it, my role

In between takes for 'Gorgeous'

ended up getting enlarged during the shooting. Jackie was choreographing a major fight scene in a warehouse for the finale to show his choreography in action, but for various reasons I was asked to do the fight scene. It was a great experience and also an honour to represent Jackie in the fight scene.

ML: *In 1998, Jackie made his real American debut when he teamed with Chris Tucker and director Brett Ratner for the incredibly successful Rush Hour. Did you work on the film?*

BA: Yes and no. Finishing work on Who Am I? in Malaysia, I was told that Jackie was going to bring me out to America to work on Rush Hour. Later I was told the American union wouldn't allow it. But they did shoot a small part of the film in Hong Kong and I worked on that, rigging only.

ML: *After Rush Hour's phenomenal success, Jackie lept into production of his next movie Gorgeous, co-starring the lovely Shu Qi. For this film, Jackie pulled you into the spotlight*

as his martial arts nemesis for the film. Can you tell us about the film?

BA: It's a romantic comedy, a change of pace for Jackie but there is still some good action. A business rival of Jackie's, actor/singer Emil Chau (the ice-cream seller from Rumble in the Bronx and Mr. Nice Guy), wants to discredit Jackie. So he hires me to challenge Jackie to a fight. We have our first fight on a roof carpark and I manage to beat Jackie. He goes off and trains for a rematch and we have a big end fight at a processing factory.

ML: *While you've worked with Jackie for several movies now, previously it's been little bits of action, group action and small sections of one on one. How did you feel going one on one twice! with Jackie for this film?*

BA: It's really amazing. They threw me a real curveball, my contract refers to me as an actor rather than a stuntman. And I've never really done any acting before. It was all new but an opportunity like this doesn't come along very often, and when it does, you can't turn it down.

I was given the chance to face off and do battle one on one in two fight scenes with the greatest action movie star of my time. It's wild, it is such a great opportunity that I know a lot of people would like to have. And the fights are somewhat different to anything Jackie's done previously. Both fights aren't to the death, we both use some powerful techniques and a lot of flashy moves but they're set up like gentlemen's bouts. We both wear boxing gloves and we're not trying to kill each other.

ML: *Looking back at Gorgeous now, what is your opinion of the film? How do you rate the film as a whole, the action scenes, and your performance?*

BA: Well I think that this film is very different from anything Jackie has done before. It is not really an action movie, although it does have action. Judging by the reviews in Asia I don't think that the American audience will be too disappointed, at least I hope not.

I think the action scenes are OK for the kind of movie that it is. I still think that the action in Drunken Master 2 is superior, but then again we spent just under two weeks filming both fight scenes, whereas in Drunken Master 2 the end fight alone took just under three months to film!

Sam Wong (longtime Jackie Chan stunt team member, the Chinese Police Kung Fu Guy from Police Story 3: Supercop and one of Van Damme's doubles for most of Double Team) is officially listed as choreographer for the film, but Jackie has still got a lot of input and the final say on things. And that's one of the things I most admire about Jackie, he has such a brilliant mind and is so creative. I love working with him, and being around him when he's creating action, it is amazing. It really is a case of seeing a master at work.

For myself I don't think it's the best action I'm capable of, but I'm always hard on myself. I think it's up to the audience to tell me if the action is good or not. But I hope people will like what they see, Jackie pulls off some nice moves and it's good to see him in a one on one fight even if it's with me! Acting wise, I still have a long way to go.

ML: *Following Gorgeous, you did stunts on Gen-X Cops for Media Asia choreographed by Nicky Li, before production began on Jackie's eagerly awaited cowboy movie/dream project Shanghai Noon. What was your job on this film, was it in front of or behind the camera?*

BA: Shanghai Noon was filmed in Canada and China and is easily the most expensive Jackie Chan movie I have worked on. My job on this project was to assist with the action sequences as part of the Jackie Chan stunt team, rigging stunts behind the camera and doubling actors and stuntmen in front of the camera. I doubled as a Native American in one fight scene and as a cowboy in another.

ML: *How long did you work on the production for?*

BA: I think we started shooting toward the end of May 1999 in Calgary (Canada) and finished in September.

ML: *What can you tell us about the movie, in terms of cast, standout action scenes etc?*

BA: The plot concerns the kidnapping of a Chinese princess in the 1880s. She is taken to the US and ransomed. Jackie plays a member of the Royal Guard who is sent to get her back. He teams up with a cowboy played by Owen Wilson. Lucy Liu plays the princess and Roger Yuan plays the bad guy. It is a fun action movie and some of the scenes are very funny.

There is a great stunt sequence involving Jackie and a locomotive and plenty of fighting. One fight I am particularly proud of as a Wushu enthusiast involves Jackie fighting with a makeshift rope-dart. In fact we had two very talented Wushu performers from China as part of the team. Wu-Gang is the current All China Wushu Champion and a good friend, the other is a former Beijing Wushu Team member Cui Ya-Hui. They both brought so much to the action. I believe this film will be one of Jackie's best.

ML: *In Asia, Jackie has spoken of you as his first western student/disciple, how do you feel about this?*

BA: Personally I think of it as a great honour that Jackie has taken me as his student. I think any master-student relationship is very unique and special. It doesn't matter if the discipline is martial arts, painting, building or in this case action film-making; this kind of relationship shows a trust and commitment. The master may have devoted their whole life, made many sacrifices for their art. I don't think the master would bother to take on a student if he did not expect the same kind of dedication. Jackie makes the best action films in the world today and has been no.1 at the Asian box-office for 20 years. He always expects excellence. So it is also a great responsibility for me.

ML: *So what's next for Brad Allan?*

BA: Well, I am living in Hong Kong right now training and studying Cantonese.

I have just returned from Shanghai working on my own project, a Wushu instructional tape that I hope to release in the near future. I have put a lot of effort into it and have found some top level Wushu athletes and coaches to help me. I really believe that there is a lot of interest in Wushu in the US, not to mention talent. Wushu has helped me to achieve so much and my aim is to help raise the level of the sport. Providing quality instruction is the first step. I know that there are numerous martial art and Wushu instructional videos available, but my research has shown that there are very few that explain, clearly, the essential training methods used by all elite level Wushu athletes in China today.

I am also preparing to start work on Jackie's next film project for director Teddy Chen (Downtown Torpedoes, Purple Storm) entitled Spy City. This film will be shot on location in Korea, Istanbul and Hong Kong, and by all accounts is going to be action packed.

ML: *Thanks for talking to me Brad, any last words?*

BA: I'd like to say thanks to a few people. First and foremost, a very big thank you to Mr. Jackie Chan. He's been my inspiration, the biggest influence on me, and has done so much for me, he's always been true to his word and he's made so many of my dreams come true.

I'd also like to say thanks to my Mum and Dad for all of their support and encouragement. Thanks to my coaches Liang Chang-Xing and Tang Lai-Wei.

Thanks to all of Jackie's stunt team - Nicky Li, Sam Wong, Man Ching, Andy Cheng, Rocky, Mars. They are like my family, they accepted me as a member and a brother and that's how I think of all of them. And to anyone else who's ever helped me or inspired me, thank you.

JACKIE CHAN

GORGEOUS

ACTION HAS NEVER LOOKED THIS GOOD.

PROMOTIONAL COPY NOT FOR SALE OR RENT

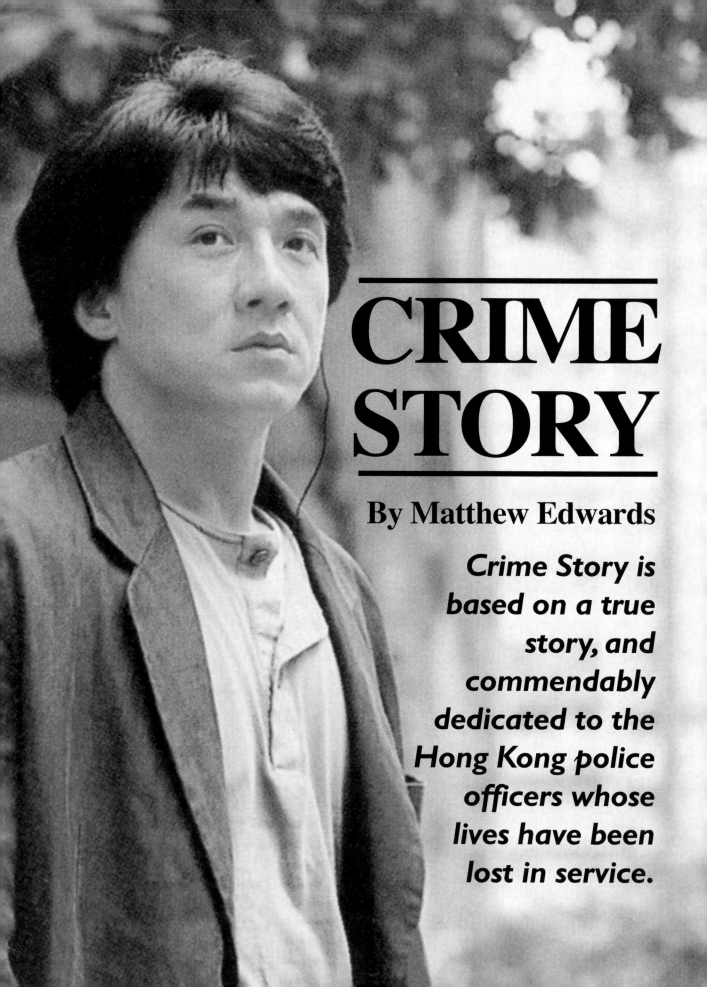

CRIME STORY

By Matthew Edwards

Crime Story is based on a true story, and commendably dedicated to the Hong Kong police officers whose lives have been lost in service.

Any doubts about the credentials of Jackie's acting ability would surely be dispelled by Kirk Wong's Crime Story. However, this is not your typical Jackie Chan movie. The feel of the film is more sombre, representing a refreshing change of pace, without being dismissive of Jackie's usual output. The fight sequences here are more spasmodic and realistic, exploding after moments of calm. This serves to heighten their impact. Crime Story is a serious movie, raising serious questions.

Impeccably directed by Kirk Wong, his anti-bureaucracy attitude lends a certain new dimension to a Jackie Chan production. Muted and restrained in comparison with Wong's usual Peninsula thrillers, it represses the chance of any occurence of the slapstick elements and motifs usually employed in the fabric of Jackie's movies. Despite this, Crime Story stands remarkably on its own, and rates as one of the best thrillers to emerge from Hong Kong in the last decade.

Crime Story is based on a true story, and commendably dedicated to the Hong Kong police officers whose lives have been lost in service. When a real-estate billionaire is kidnapped and held to ransom, Jackie is the cop assigned to track down the kidnappers, unaware that his partner Hung (Kent Cheng) is one of them. Outfoxed at every turn, the film is propelled towards a tense and bloody conclusion, with the fate of the victim solely in Jackie's hands.

Crime Story begins at an electric pace. Against a backdrop of abandoned warehouses, a soaring and stylish high speed car chase ensues, culminating in a frenzied smash and grab pile up. The intensity of the scene is enhanced by Wong's positioning of cameras in and outside of the vehicles. This simulates the impact of the vehicles slamming into one another to greater effect, giving the viewer a sharpened experience of the carnage unfolding.

What transpires is a practice attempt at the kidnap of wealthy businessman Mr Wong. The rehearsals over-riding failure causes bickering, as the would-be kidnappers emerge dazed and bruised. Here we are introduced to Hung, who stresses the need for more efficiency when kidnapping Wong.

Told in flashback, the next scene introduces us to Inspector Chan (Chan). A psychological counsellor discusses with Jackie a shooting incident where he was responsible for the death of an innocent citizen. Consumed with guilt, Jackie recollects the events leading up to the shooting of the civilian. This is presented in a sucession of quick, sharp excursions into excessive violence.

Four heist members begin firing aimlessly at civilians within a crowded market. People flee in panic, the camera acting more as an observer. The film's style has an edgy cluttered feel with its hand-held documentary approach. Caught in the shooting, a pregnant woman is dragged to safety by Jackie, before fulfilling his duties. The gang begin to shoot up an oncoming police vehicle, whereupon Jackie steps in blowing one hood away, his body flung backwards in slow-motion into a nearby shop window.

The gang's attention turns towards Jackie, and in between some skilfully handled stunts, one blistering scene stands out. Jackie covers behind a series of parked cars, whereupon the gang proceeds to sling a grenade underneath a vehicle, sending the car upwards and Jackie diving to the ground. This is followed by another great stunt which sees Jackie becoming trapped between two vehicles, before jumping from one to the next, blasting away the gang, unfortunately also an innocent citizen.

The strength of the scene without doubt lies in the shattering violence inter-cutting between Jackie's counselling session. This is an effective tool, presenting the violence in smaller segments, creating a more realised impact. The frenzied pace adds to the confusion developing on screen. Kirk Wong shows the shooting realistically without glamour. The violence here is more visceral. It is presented accurately, as hectic and messy, unlike the opera-esque Woo, where everything is staged in relation to the scene.

Through the confusion Jackie must act without fully

realising the implications of his actions. They are based on instinct alone. Locals going about their daily business get caught in the crossfire. Crashes seem unavoidable. The fight sequences possess no choreography it seems. It is chaotic, almost accidental. There seems to be no rhythm to the violence. Wong's characters are acting on instinct rather than judgement. Chan is not acting on bravura. He is simply doing his job.

Jackie becomes assigned to the case of Mr Wong, who suspects he is a kidnap target. Having already been kidnapped once before, Chan suggests he is becoming paranoid about those he is unfamiliar with. Despite reassurances, Jackie is instructed to protect Wong, doing so when called upon to break up a demonstration from disgruntled workers.

It is at this stage when the story kicks into action with the kidnap of Mr Wong. Reclining in her seat,

Wong's wife complains of heart trouble. Wong catches a glimpse of a car tracking his own within his rear-view mirror. Panicking he contacts Chan, who quickly dismisses it. However he decides to leave his prior engagement as he feels he has a duty to protect Wong.

With their cover blown the kidnappers pull down their masks, sparking into action. An enthralling chase erupts with the kidnappers' cars hurtling into Wong's. Moving side by side of Wong's vehicle, one member from each car produces a giant steel claw, which are smashed through Wong's windows, clamping the cars together. Clambering through the window, they bind and gag Wong and his wife, with Hung insisting on the wellbeing of his wife, as she's the one who will pay the ransom.

Spotting the kidnappers, Jackie gives chase. Played out within tight narrow streets, the kidnappers force

Jackie off the road, his vehicle over-turning as it slides into an embankment. What unfolds is a truly breath taking scene, which epitomises the extraordinary lengths he will go to. Wong again employing the documentary approach, creates a vivid and realistic enactment, as we witness Jackie kicking open his windscreen, freeing himself from the confines of his car. Chan then proceeds to overturn his de-railed car, leaving the viewer to beg the question, "Is there anything this man can't do?"

Climbing back into his vehicle, Jackie goes full throttle crashing through a barrier, in what begins a death defying stunt where his car is seen descending down a near vertical drop. Swerving back onto the main road, Jackie pursues the kidnappers, meanwhile emptying a bottle of water over his blood soaked eye. At this point Hung's kidnapping plan turns into murder when they cruelly and despicably run over a police motorcyclist, killing him instantly. Anxiety creeps in as the kidnappers lose control, suddenly turning coldly on another police motorcyclist, knocking him from his bike; injured on the floor, one of the kidnappers attempts to run the police officer over. Jackie, realising the danger, reverses into the kidnappers' car, blocking their path. Consequently the two vehicles collide, spiralling in tandem with the floored police officer into a barrier, firmly locking him against it. The kidnappers escape, as Jackie rushes to the aid of his colleague who lies critically ill on the ground.

Picking up his motorcycle, Jackie takes the injured officer to hospital, escorted by the Hong Kong Police Division. It's great here to see Jackie riding a motorcycle, weaving and turning through the streets of Hong Kong, before carrying the officer into the emergency ward. There's an interesting and bizarre scene directly after which consists of Wong's wife being brought back to life with the jump leads of a revved up car. Only in Hong Kong it seems can these things happen.

Chan organises a team to catch the kidnappers, but is continually outfoxed by Hung, who hinders and sabotages the efforts of

the police department. During a failed stakeout, they find a lead linking the kidnap to a Mr Ting, thus taking both Chan and Hung to Taiwan, with Hung insisting to Chan that they should treat it as a vacation. Once there the Taiwan police instruct Chan and Hung that they are merely there as observers, and therefore are not involved in helping secure the suspect's apprehension.

Disobeying orders the pair head off to Ting's hideout, where the Taiwan police mount an undercover bust. Blowing through the apartment's wall the raid begins as riot police open fire on Ting's men. Ting escapes into the crowded streets until cornered off by the police. Ting flees to the roof pursued by Jackie. Now the shootout intensifies as the police and gang members battle it out in a brutal rooftop brawl. Picking up an Uzi, Jackie fires on Ting and his men. What unfolds is a wonderful scene in which Ting's men throw explosives which bring a huge neon advertising board crashing down

only feet away from Jackie. Sliding down the shattered advertising board he follows Ting into a cinema.

Filmed above the cinema, this sequence has all the trademarks of a Jackie Chan fight, except again on a grittier level. After beating one member, Jackie faces one thug armed with a knife. Dodging a few swipes, Jackie employs a lightning kick, sending the thug tumbling downwards into an array of cabinets. The same fate happens to a few other members, before a mini duel with Ting takes place. Armed with a broken headlamp, Ting attempts to knock Chan from the rafters. Successfully defending Ting's vain attacks, Chan kicks Ting into a layer of fluorescent netting. Ting is entangled, but Hung comes to his rescue by hitting Chan on the back of the head with a plank of wood. Hung tries to free Ting, but when Ting becomes trapped he threatens to spill everything he knows, forcing

Hung to push him off the roof's exterior, all under the recovering eyes of Chan. Although both are sent back off to Hong Kong disgraced for disobeying orders, Chan's prime suspect is now Hung.

After an excellent fight sequence in the police department, Chan's investigation leads him to an abandoned ship off shore. A search of the vessel for Wong begins, and ends in a confrontation between Hung and Chan in the cargo hold. After saving Hung from a near death situation, Hung turns on Chan, sending him down to the lower confines of the ship. Dazed and bruised, Jackie searches for an exit. In order to frame Chan, Hung turns his gun on himself. Surfacing in the choppy waters alongside the ship, Jackie is detained.

Whilst Chan protests his innocence, Hung moves proceedings along with Mrs Wong in relation to the ransom request. Chan convinces his superiors of Hung's involvement, thus setting the scene for an

'Crime Story' - *Jackie's serious movie*

epic finale. Camping outside Hung's potential hideout, Chan spots members of his gang. Whilst attempting to inform his counterparts, one member surprises Chan and attacks him with a spade! A blistering, weirdly funny and agonising set-piece unravels. This is Chan excelling in familiar territory. This awesome fight is stylised to perfection, as Chan defends himself against flying chairs and the deranged spade man. A gunman also approaches Chan, who quickly slams a fridge into the gunman, before wrestling his hand into a deep fat fryer! Chan brilliantly disposes of one attacker by electrocuting him, then oddly he fishes the gun out of the fryer, and begins shooting down Hung's men!

Hung emerges, only to ignite the building. The building soon becomes a towering inferno, as Hung desperately attempts to escape. In the ensuing madness one gunman is burnt alive after attempting to shoot Jackie. A gas leak increases the tension as the deterioration of the building speeds up. Killing two more of Hung's henchmen, we are left with a final showdown between Hung and Chan. Chan severely beats Hung, and tries to extract from him the whereabouts of Wong. Hung repents, forcing Chan to handcuff Hung. But when Chan becomes distracted by the sound of a trapped child, Hung again escapes, but in doing so receives divine retribution, as he falls through the building's weakened interior. Chan discovers Hung de-mobilised under a block of concrete. Attempting to free Hung, he tells Chan to save himself and the child, before redeeming himself by disclosing the whereabouts of Wong. Just as Chan escapes the building explodes.

With the discovery of Wong, there is an emotional reunion with his wife, as the Chinese police hand Wong over to Hong Kong officials. Chan's determination is commended, before he quietly leaves, burning all records of the case.

Crime Story sees Jackie in awesome form, and it is no surprise that he won the best actor award at the Golden Horse film awards. His presence is captivating, oozing with charisma. Although the film is at times shockingly violent, the film is a remarkable testament to a distinguished career, proving how versatile his abilities are. There seem to be no limits when it comes to Jackie's movies,

and for this he must be commended. Credit should also be handed to Kirk Wong who has also made the transition to Hollywood. His detailed eye towards urban violence and corruption is on a par with that of Lam. His documentary approach is exhilarating, adding a certain freakishness to the picture. His fight sequences are brutal, but never become indulged in glamorising the villains. It is a film that should be viewed subjectively and deserves to be taken very much on face value.

Factoids:

The original script for Crime Story was written by Purple Storm and Accidental Spy director Teddy Chen.

Crime Story director Kirk Wong made his Hollywood directorial debut with the action comedy The Big Hit in 1998. The film starred Mark Wahlberg who trained for his role with none other than Wheels on Meals/Dragons Forever supervillain Benny Urquidez.

Crime Story originally began production with a strangely hairstyled Jet Li in the lead, but he left the project soon after filming started, and Jackie stepped in and won a Golden Horse Award for Best Actor for his efforts.

Bad guys in the movie include Kent Cheng Chut-sze perhaps better known for his ongoing role as Butcher Wing in the Once Upon A Time in China series, Wing Chun maestro Stephen Chan, actor stuntmen James Ha, Chung Fa and of course Ken Low Wai-kwong.

The robbers at the beginning of the movie include Sam Wong and Mars...

OUT OF THE VAULTS:

JACKIE CHAN PULLING NO PUNCHES REVISITED!!!

Looking back in time: A young Mike Leeder interviews the main man in 95.

It's hard to believe it now, with Jackie's success at the international box office with Rumble in the Bronx and Rush Hour, and the mass acceptance of Jackie Chan as a cultural icon, but a few short years ago Jackie Chan was still a cult hero, or as Ian Johnston put it, "a cult waiting to be cultivated." This was a time when Jackie's movies were sadly too often relegated to video only releases, with little mainstream distribution. Screen Power's Mike Leeder takes us back to a time just before Jackie's much deserved international breakthrough in the following interview.

When our illustrious editor and publisher Richard Cooper (a.k.a. The Kid) asked me if he could run this interview for Screen Power I was a bit reluctant. The interview had previously run in slightly edited formats in Combat magazine and the April 1997 edition of Inside Kung Fu's Martial Arts Legends (by the way if anyone has a spare copy of it, I'd be most grateful, someone at Golden Harvest took my last one!) and a German martial arts magazine. I didn't want people to accuse me of rehashing old material, but Richard explained that it was pretty much the last really in-depth interview anyone had conducted with Jackie in the west, before the runaway success of Rumble in the Bronx brought him that much more success.

So I sat back down and re-read the interview myself for the first time in a long-time and casting my ego aside, I do have to admit that I think it's a pretty good interview. Jackie was in the greatest of spirits that day I recall. Upon his arrival at the JC Group headquarters he sent his assistants away and moved the interview location from the lounge to his inner sanctum upstairs.

Jackie was fresh, open, energetic, and more than willing to go into detail as we discussed his career, even to the point of extending the time granted to me, and going on to invite myself and my very good friend actor/stuntman Michael Miller (a.k.a. Tickler from Knock Off) who was serving as my photographer that day, to attend the premiere of Rumble in the Bronx as his guests a few days later.

So sit back and pour yourself a nice drink as I take you back to early 1995, when Jackie was still a cult waiting to be cultivated (and I had a lot more hair)! and enjoy part one of the complete version of Pulling No Punches Revisited!

Mike Leeder:

Jackie, you released Drunken Master 2 to great success both domestically and internationally. The film was the sequel to the classic Seasonal Films release Drunken Master directed by Yuen Woo-ping (who recently choreographed the superb action sequences in The Matrix), the film that cemented your success, and it was probably one of the most eagerly anticipated sequels of all time. When Wushu maestro and stuntman Bruce Fontaine and I spent a couple of days on the set in late 1993, the film's original director Lau Chia-liang had just left the film over creative differences and you had taken over the directorial reins. You told us how you were working hard to make the film the very best you could, while so many people were implying that the film was out of control and would fail at the box office. The film was of course a huge success with audiences and critics worldwide. Looking back at the film now, are you happy with it?

Jackie Chan:

Not really! (laughing) Of course I am happy that the film was very successful at the box office but to tell the truth I am not one hundred percent satisfied with the film. If from the very beginning I had been the director myself, then it would have been a better film and very different in style to the released version. If I am only the actor in a film, I have time to do other things, so I invited Lau Chia-liang to direct. He was a very good director, and when I spoke to him about the project, I could see that he wanted to make a good film too. Unfortunately, I don't think that his directing style is up-to-date, the film looks like an old movie.

I wasn't always in China during some of the early stages of filming; I had to take care of several other things, so a lot of the footage was shot without me seeing it. I had very high expectations of Lau Chia-liang, so later when I saw the footage I was very disappointed and thought that the film wouldn't do well at the

firing him, pushing him off the film.

JC: No, it was the HKSA's decision. They asked me to take over and truthfully, when the movie came out, if it hadn't been a success who would people blame? What would people say is the reason for its failure? First, is me, then Golden Harvest who released the film, then the HKSA and lastly Lau Chia-liang. So the HKSA spoke to Lau Chia-liang, and I set to work re-shooting and re-working the film. Lau had over 9,000 feet of completed film; I cut

box office and the audience would be very disappointed. But out of respect for Lau Chia-liang, I didn't say anything and we continued filming.

Mike, you know this film was being made for the Hong Kong Stuntman's Association (HKSA), but when the HKSA Board of Directors saw the film, they were shocked, they said that there was no way they could release the film as it was. I suggested that maybe if they let me re-edit some scenes, re-work certain parts of the plot and film some fresh scenes maybe we could salvage the film, so they [the HKSA Board] sat down with Lau Chia-liang and told him that they weren't satisfied with the film. But it's not like they were firing him.

ML: *It's strange, because certain elements of both the Hong Kong press and some western magazines and writers tried to accuse you of*

4,000 feet, and re-shot, re-dubbed, re-worked and re-edited for the next few months. Now I know that Lau Chia-liang wasn't happy with the situation, but it wasn't my fault. Then he announced to everybody that he was going to make Drunken Master 3 his way, to show people the real joi kuen (Drunken Boxing), to show his way of doing things. That makes me feel a bit strange, Drunken Master 2 still lists his name as director, and when it was released and did well everybody had a very high opinion of his work. Then when his Drunken Master 3 comes out, what happens? It fails at the box office, the audience didn't like it and their opinion of Lau Chia-liang changed.

ML: *One thing that really impressed me and a lot of other people about the film was that the fight choreography for Drunken Master 2 was so crisp and clear. After so many kung fu/swordplay movies where everyone was flying around and the action was all just quick cuts and very confusing, your action was stylised but still realistic. You only used wires a few times and then merely to enhance the action.*

JC: (laughing) Exactly! That's why I spend a long time on the action for this film. Too often Hong Kong films go crazy with the action, I remember going to a film festival in Paris two

wanted to make Drunken Master 2 for a long time, and when the revival in the kung fu movie came about, I thought it might be time. But when we were making the film, everybody else's kung fu movies started dying at the box office and people were saying that I had missed the boat, that it was too late. But I don't think so... if I make a good film, then I think the audience will come to see it.

ML: *You proved that with Drunken Master 2's success. I was surprised that nobody has tried*

JC speaks out in his private room at The JC Group office

years ago, where many people asked me, "Why can everybody fly in Hong Kong movies?" It's very stupid! When I watch a lot of Hong Kong films, I don't know what the hell is going on! It's all quick cuts and moves too fast. All the action is doubles, not even stunt doubles, but just body doubles! When the actor comes to the set it's just for one or two hours and they just sit down and do close-ups. Or like this! (Mimes playing a harp, dispatching darts against numerous enemies, complete with noises.) Then you cut to explosions and stuntmen reacting. I see this kind of action and wonder why they don't use weapons like these in modern warfare! (laughing) It's really stupid!

And even more crazy is that even though these people can fly, they still ride horses half the time. If you can fly, fly, don't ride a horse and then fly! I look at this kind of film and think that people outside of Hong Kong will dismiss all Hong Kong films as rubbish. You know I've

to copy the style of action since its release.

JC: They want to! I am not the best action actor in Asia, but I am lucky for a couple of reasons. One is that I love making movies, so I take care to produce good ones, and also I am very lucky to have Raymond Chow and Golden Harvest behind me, willing to support me. Did you know that just for the scene in the foundry, we spent a couple of months filming this scene? Most companies do not have the time to spend on their productions, and too many actors make too many movies at the same time and can't give the time to one production. As for me, because of my support, I can spend one day for one shot! (laughing) I'm not so young anymore; I can jump about six feet in the air, but only for a few takes. After five or six takes, I can't jump that high anymore, so I stop and do some other shots. Then later or the next day, I will try to do that movement again. So many companies haven't got the time or money, they have to finish the whole scene today, so often they will end up doing a stupid wire shot that's unbelievable just to finish, and that's why they end up with bad movies so often.

ML: *I understand what you're saying Jackie, I've been on a lot of sets where time has been in very short supply. I remember being on the set of The Moon Warriors, and everybody was rushing to finish the film that night because the film was previewing six days later!*

JC: You know it! The quality of a film is very important. For Rumble in the Bronx, after we finished the film, we took it to Australia to do the Dolby sound and then to America for the music. We try to make it the best film we can, while a lot of Hong Kong companies try to make their films the worst they possibly can! They look at everything as short-term return and end up destroying themselves. Right now Hong Kong films are losing to western films in Hong Kong for the second year running and the whole market in Asia for Hong Kong films is down. Even big films like God of Gamblers 2/The Return of the God of Gamblers with Chow Yun-fat and Fist of Legend with Jet Lee aren't doing well in other Asian countries, even in Korea! (Mike Factoid: Korea has traditionally been one of the greatest markets for Hong Kong action movies, with distributors buying action films unseen, especially any film with Jackie, Chow Yun-fat, Jet Lee, Cynthia Khan etc. However in the last year even this market has changed, and now both audiences and distributors are responding only to high quality action films.) Have you seen the Jet Lee film, Mike?

ML: *Yes, but I thought it was very uneven. The fight scenes don't gel with the dramatic parts of the film very well, and the action is way too fast. There is no denying the talent of Jet Lee, Chin Siu-ho and Billy Chow or Yuen Woo-ping, but the action just gets too fast and detracts from the techniques and their abilities.*

JC: Yes, it's too fast! Why? Because the action director has been given too much control over the fight scenes instead of liasing with the director. Gordon Chan is a very good dramatic director, but for the action scenes he isn't on the set and Yuen Woo-ping has complete control for this section. The scene takes a few days to shoot, and a couple of days later Gordon Chan comes back. That's why there is a bad mix between the tone of the film's dramatic scenes and action scenes. That's wrong. On my films, no matter who the director is, I will spend as much time as possible on the set. From my own experience, I have found that nobody can really direct me by themselves. On Crime Story and Rumble in the Bronx for example, I'm always on the set, maybe more than the official director! (laughing) I co-direct most of my films. If the film does badly it reflects upon me, so I try to take care of my career.

ML: *Well, you seem to be doing a good job of it. If you look at the Hong Kong film industry over the last ten years or so, you are pretty much the only stable consistent figure, so your strategy must be working.*

JC: (Shakes his head) You know that everybody always says to me, "Jackie, you're a miracle! You are still at the top, your films are still making money. How can you do this?" I tell them it's not a miracle, it's the fact that I care about my career. There's one action actor that I know, he's very successful at the moment but seems to be losing his appeal. One time he was filming two separate films at Golden Harvest at the same time, and one day it called for him to shoot two major action scenes, over the same days. (laughing) I've done this before due to scheduling problems, like on City Hunter, Crime Story and Supercop where I was sleeping travelling between locations and then catching a few more hours at my office. But this guy is different, he comes into my office and tells me how tired he is and ends up sleeping on my sofa. I go to both sets and he had stunt doubles doing all of his action for him. When I go back to my office and talk to him, he tells me that there is no need for him to do all the action, he can let the stuntmen do it and just do a close-up here and there. I thought about all my injuries and wondered for a moment if he had the right idea, but both of his films died at the box office and then I know that I am right, you have to take care of your films. People expect to see me doing action, I can't just do a close-up here and there! Take care of your movie for all the markets. Look at the current Hong Kong releases. God of Gamblers 2 with Chow Yun-fat is doing very well in Hong Kong but is failing overseas.

ML: *But even in Hong Kong, it's not doing as well as it first seems. The film has a built in audience wanting to see Chow reprise his character after so long, but the film disappoints and they raised the ticket prices just for this movie.*

JC: (laughing) I'm glad you understand the Hong Kong way of doing business, it's sad because all they are doing is fooling or lying to themselves when they inflate the box office figures. I always tell my crew that it's bad enough if you lie to other people, but if you lie to yourself it's really stupid! OK if you tell the truth then maybe people won't always like what you say, but they will believe it and respect you for your honesty. That's my philosophy, if someone asks me a question, I tell them the truth about what I feel. Yesterday I was told that I was going to receive an award for Best Asian Actor in some ceremony. The press asked me how I felt. I told them the truth, you give me an award, of course I feel happy, especially if it's an award that really means something. In Hong Kong for instance, you have four major radio stations and they all have separate awards ceremonies which I understand, but they give awards to everybody. It's stupid, I give an award to you Mike, then so your friend Michael Miller

doesn't get upset I give an award to him too, and then another one to myself just to make us all feel happy. It makes the awards worthless. If I was to win an Oscar, the Academy Award of course I would feel so happy and proud, because there is only one Oscar and it's accepted worldwide as an official award for your achievement, it's special, it means something. But if LA had its own Oscars, and then New York, and then London, and then Hong Kong, it wouldn't mean anything. Give people an award that really means something, not just to make them feel so happy.

ML: *Something else that Drunken Master 2 proved without a doubt, is that you're still in incredible physical condition and can perform some incredible martial artistry. In the west a lot of people had cited the lack of fight scenes in Supercop and Crime Story as proof that you were trying to get away from martial arts as you got older and couldn't perform them anymore. Drunken Master 2 certainly silenced those critics. Did you have to do a lot of special martial arts training to get back into form?*

JC: No! (laughing) Yes, of course I did a lot of training for the film, and it's one of the reasons why I didn't want to direct it. That's not saying that I wasn't willing to have any input or say-so in the film. But having someone else direct does allow me a few luxuries, I can spend

more time training and perhaps even have a social life. (laughing) When I am directing on my own, I take control of the casting, locations, editing, the soundtrack, everything and it takes me about two years to do each film. As for training, it all depends on the film, its time setting and the style, to being comical, non stop action or dramatic. If I'm doing a Drunken Master movie I will spend a lot of time training in traditional kung fu. You know that I have my own ideas concerning a third Drunken Master movie, not Lau Chia-liang's one but my official sequel. The positive reaction around the world tells me that there is still a market for good Drunken Master style movies. But I'm still working on the storyline, I want the third one to go in a new direction. If you look at Drunken Master with Yuen Woo-ping, the storyline is very simple, drinking, fighting, drinking, fighting, comedy and that's about it, not much real depth. For part two, we have a more adult storyline that you shouldn't drink too much and mix it with a story about stolen treasure. But for part three I want to take it further, I have several ideas but I've not finalised anything yet. But when I do and before we can film then it's back to all of this (Jackie starts laughing, humming the Wong Fei-hung theme, Under Generals Orders, and jumping around the room doing a variety of traditional kung fu styles ending with Drunken Boxing as he drops back into his chair).

I watch a lot of modern day Hong Kong movies and people are driving cars, firing machine guns but when they fight, they do this (Jackie adopts Choy Li-fut and Wushu poses). It's very stupid! It's like an old kung fu movie! (laughing) In a modern movie, you should be more rough and ready like this (Jackie starts throwing punches, kicks and elbows at my head!). When I made Operation Condor, I had to fight a lot of western actors and stuntmen, Bruce Fontaine and Kenn Goodman are two of the best western martial artists I have worked with, they're very versatile and are two of the few who can really handle Hong Kong action. But much to their disappointment, I had to tell them that they weren't meant to be great kung fu guys, but mercenaries with some martial arts training. They can both do a lot of Chinese martial arts and acrobatics, but I wanted them to look rough like streetfighters, real fighters,

not martial artists. When I watch a modern day film and people are fighting with very traditional kung fu movements, too much of the time it doesn't make any sense. The problem is that too often the fight choreographer will get full control of the fight scene instead of a co-operation between director and action director. This can lead to problems when the fights don't match the tone of the film. But by the time the director realises it's too late to fix it. That's why I work very closely with my directors, (laughing) maybe too closely!

ML: *That's probably why most of your films have a very steady even feel to them. The action flows with the story.*

JC: I take care of my movies, because everything I have now is because of my movies. If my movies fail, then no audience, no fans, no money, no business. That's why I care, movies are my life! Right now I'm choosing which project to do next. Stanley Tong has a movie about the CIA he wants me to do (this would later become Jackie Chan's First Strike, Police Story 4, Final Project), or I might be working with Sammo Hung again on a new project (Mr. Nice Guy), or I might be making a racing movie with Gordon Chan (Thunderbolt). I want to choose another strong project but I haven't made any decision yet.

ML: *I was very surprised that while Michael Ho Sung-pak (the original Lu K'ang from the Mortal Kombat video game, and later of WMAC Masters fame) worked on Drunken Master 2 for so long, he didn't really end up doing anything. When I spoke with him on the set, he told me that he was finding Hong Kong choreography difficult to relate to, and in the finished film quite a bit of the action his character performs is actually done by Sam Wong (long-time JC stuntman, the red-vested kung fu army superior from Supercop).*

JC: (Nodding) Yes, actually I didn't cast Michael Ho, he was playing one of the turtles in Teenage Mutant Ninja Turtles 3 when Lau Chia-liang was working on the film, and Lau was impressed by Michael and invited him to Hong Kong and gave him the major role in Drunken Master 2. I didn't doubt Lau's judgement so I didn't ask to see what Michael could do; we were holding him back for the big fight at the finale. Then after Lau left the project and we started working on the finale, we knew it was a mistake. Mike, you know that for Hong Kong fighting there is a rhythm, it's not just one or two moves and cut, but it's also not a steady continuous pace. We go up and down, breaking some sections into one, two, three, and others into one through thirty, you have to be able to go up and down with the rhythm. Michael Ho just couldn't catch the rhythm. It doesn't mean that he's not a very good martial artist, he is. But movie fighting is very different, especially Hong Kong style. He couldn't catch the flavour. So I changed the ending, with Michael doing fewer moves, and we were able to finish him up quite quickly, which left Ken Low Wai-kwong and me. I told Ken that this was a big showcase for him, and that he had to work on being as flexible as possible so we could have a wild fight scene. (laughing) Poor Ken, every day for one whole month he was stretching, doing the splits, everyday, everywhere, even when he is sleeping! (laughing) I think this movie made him cry. You look at the end fight though, it took two months to shoot and it was very good, forget Van Damme, Ken shows what kicking is about.

ML: In the west, there is currently a trend for releasing director's cuts of movies with re-instated footage, deleted scenes etc. As we've mentioned, so much footage was shot and later removed from Drunken Master 2, would you ever consider releasing a director's cut, a revised version of Drunken Master 2?

JC: No, I only take footage out if it doesn't work, so to put any footage back would only make the film worse. A lot of the footage we deleted was Lau Chia-liang's interpretation of Joi Kuen (Drunken Boxing). Lau doesn't like Drunken Boxing; he wants it to be more like real kung fu. In his mind, Drunken Boxing should be like this (Jackie demonstrates one drunken movement, in this case a punch, before dropping back to normal), somebody tries to hit you, then you become drunk for the block or the strike and then go back to normal. I know my version of Drunken Boxing is not real kung fu, but the real one is boring and just doesn't look good on film, while my version looks good. That's why we had to do so many re-shoots for a lot of scenes, because Lau's views and mine are very different. You know the scene at the end when I read the message on the fan, and it inspires me to win the fight. Well we had already shot the fight scene with Vincent Tuatane in the foundry with the fan, and didn't want to re-shoot it. So I spent a lot of time thinking of a reason why I would carry a fan into battle, and then I thought if it has a message that could inspire me to change my strategy, then I can use it. And after I finished all the re-shoots and presented the HKSA with my version of Drunken Master 2, they gave me a standing ovation. I am very happy that both the HKSA and the audience are so happy with the film.

ML: Prior to Drunken Master 2, you made the dark edged drama Crime Story for director Kirk Wong (of The Big Hit fame). The film really gave you a chance to stretch your acting skills. Your character is haunted by inner demons and both attracted to and repelled by the violence he encounters. How did you first get involved in the film?

JC: When I was filming Twin Dragons, Kirk was playing the main villain. One day he started telling me about this film he wanted to make about a real kidnapping case in Hong Kong a few years ago. It sounded very interesting but at that time I had no room in my schedule, and he'd just signed Jet Lee to play the lead. A few months later, I saw Kirk at Golden Harvest and he looked very depressed. He told me that he was having a lot of problems with the film, and that Jet Lee had walked off the film and the production was going to close. I said to him and my production crew that I was interested in taking over the lead role and completing the film but due to my schedule we would have to shoot the film in-between other projects (at this point Jackie was shooting Police Story 3: Supercop and City Hunter at the same time, with Crime Story slotting in as the third movie, resulting in a stretched out shooting schedule of almost 2 years!), which is why the film took so long to complete.

ML: I like the film, you took a very big risk with such a dramatic role. Although the film wasn't the biggest box office smash of the year it did quite well, and your performance was vindicated when you won your second Golden Horse Award as Best Actor for the film. Did you find it more difficult to play such a serious role?

JC: No, it was a lot easier because I was just acting and (laughing) I wasn't being expected to fight every day. It wasn't as painful as some of my movies! The fighting and stunts are getting more difficult now, I have to try and top the previous one. I don't think that there is anyone left for me to fight anymore. I've fought Sammo Hung, Yuen Biao, Dick Wei, Billy Chow, Benny Urquidez, Bill Wallace, Ken Low. The audience always wants me to fight someone new, but who?

ML: Maybe you should fight the dinosaurs from Jurassic Park?

JC: Maybe, yes, something that isn't human, half man, half monster. That would be an interesting fight. But it's very difficult fighting all the time, acting is much easier!

Present day: JC poses in his new studio office in Sha Tin, Hong Kong.

ML: *Once again, a lot of scenes were cut from Crime Story. Including a lot of scenes with Singaporean actress Christine Ng, who played your doctor. She was in town for a long time, but is only in the film for a few short scenes, what happened?*

JC: (laughing) You know too much Mike! It's very difficult to say what happened. I like Kirk Wong and his style of filmmaking, but he wants to shoot lots of things for the film, but he doesn't know how to do it. A lot of the scenes with me and Christine made no sense, they were very strange. Kirk has a New Wave style of directing, and I just don't think our styles worked very well together.

ML: *Before Crime Story, you teamed up with director Wong Jing (God of Gamblers), for the live action adaptation of the Japanese anime City Hunter. This was a film that seemed to have all the various elements to be a classic, but the film turned out to be a disappointment.*

JC: I agree, the film was not very good. It only made money because at that time City Hunter comics and anime were very popular throughout Asia, so the film had a built in audience. But I am very disappointed with the film and I know that the audience feels the same way.

ML: *Do you think that it might have been another case of your style and Wong Jing's style clashing? You are very much the perfectionist who will shoot take after take to get something exactly the way you want it, while Wong Jing, by his own admission, is a purely commercial director, he doesn't want critical success, he only wants success at the box office.*

JC: I think you're right. I didn't find it very difficult working with Wong Jing, he's one of the easiest to get along with. He doesn't mind if you change things. If I say to him, "Can I change this?" he says, "Sure!" If I say, "Can I direct this?" he'll let me do it. It's funny but a lot of the time he wasn't directing the film, it was his assistants, because Wong Jing always has so many projects going at the same time, and I wasn't there sometimes either. So his assistants would just direct the way they felt it should be.

ML: *The City Hunter concept had been such a great success in both comic book and animated form, to the point that a lot of elements had been taken by Andy Lau for his Saviour of the Soul movie, down to character names and situations. But despite your film having so many elements from the concept, and a very strong cast, the elements just didn't seem to mix.*

JC: (Nodding) I know, I was very disappointed by the film. Wong Jing is very commercial, and his films do so well at the box office, but his style is just too loose for me. People were expecting great things when Wong Jing and myself teamed up, but everybody was disappointed.

ML: *When you first announced the project, you hoped it would be the first in a series of City Hunter films, it was going to be your ongoing James Bond flavoured franchise of films.*

JC: I feel that if I had directed City Hunter, that right now we would be making a sequel to it. At first Golden Harvest was very happy with the film, it came in on schedule, under budget and did very well at the box office. But now they have realised that the market won't accept a further City Hunter film because the audience felt cheated and was very disappointed. Most of the films I have directed we have been able to make sequels to, because both the audience and the box office takings have called for them. In the next couple of years I can make Armour of God 3, Project A 3, or Police Story 4 if I want to. If you make a good strong film then you have the chance to make a sequel. That's why I try to take care of my career. You should look at your work as an investment, take care of it and it will take care of you.

ML: *Jackie, you've fought a lot of western martial arts actors in your films including Benny the Jet Urquidez, Bill Superfoot Wallace, Richard Norton, Keith Vitali and Gary Daniels. While in your films they've looked the best they've ever looked, when they return to the west and make films, they never look as good. Why do you think this is?*

JC: Choreography! Action and martial arts choreography is so important. The camera angles, the editing, the techniques, the tempo of the fight, all of these things are very important. In real life you might be the greatest martial artist or streetfighter but in the movies, if you have poor choreography and editing, and/or you don't understand how to put together a cinematic fight scene then it's not going to look good. In Hong Kong, all the action directors have a wide knowledge of different martial arts, camera angles and film speed, editing techniques etc. I know all these things because I've spent my whole life making movies, I didn't just pick them up overnight. In America they have the best special effects, the best computer and mechanical effects etc, while here in Hong Kong special effects are still very basic. But for fight scenes, America is still far behind us. They don't understand how to put together fights for films. I've worked in America and visited a lot of film sets, but so many times the action director doesn't even get to look through the camera, let alone be involved in the editing process. That's not good, if you have an editor who doesn't understand the tempo, or doesn't understand the fight scene the way it's been shot, then he's not going to be able to make sense of it in the editing studio. The choreographer should be involved in the editing.

> *I like Stanley, he's a good friend and a good director. I did the cameo as a favour to him. If I'm in the film even just for a minute then it helps to sell the film, even if I am in drag!*

ML: *You turned up in a very interesting cameo for Stanley Tong's Project S/Once A Cop. You don't normally do cameos, so why do this one?*

JC: I like Stanley, he's a good friend and a good director. I did the cameo as a favour to him. If I'm in the film even just for a minute then it helps to sell the film, even if I am in drag! (laughing) Also, I'm on the board at Golden Harvest, so I am helping my own company. If

this film doesn't do well then maybe they will not have as much money for me to use on my next film. I want to work with Stanley again, but if this film is a flop, then Golden Harvest won't let me work with Stanley again. So I did the cameo, and they put me on the poster, and the film did OK, it wasn't a runaway hit but it didn't die at the box office.

ML: *In the past few years, you have announced several projects which have yet to be made. Could you comment on their status? Starting with Singapore Sling, Golden Harvest's proposed action comedy for the international market announced five years ago.*

JC: That one! (laughing) Golden Harvest wanted me to do another American film, but a more light hearted one, an action comedy. They were throwing names like Tom Hanks and Chevy Chase around as co-stars, but nothing was ever confirmed and truthfully I don't want to make any more American films, because the two I've done before, The Big Brawl and The Protector, not only didn't do well in America but they also didn't do well in Asia. Western audiences seem to like my Hong Kong films more than my American ones, so for now I make my films as Hong Kong international films!

ML: *Fireman's Story is one project that I know you have been wanting to do for a very long time. The first time I heard about it was when I first met you in 1990, and you spoke to me in great depth about the project. Then in the summer of 1991, the film was announced as going into production with Buddhist Fist star Tsui Siu-ming listed as director. The film was to feature little in the way of fighting, a lot of drama and emotion, combined with some incredible fire stunts. I've spoken with both top Hong Kong cinematographer Peter Pao (Misty, Saviour of the Soul, Warriors of Virtue, Bride With White Hair) and your former assistant director P'ng Kialek about the film, and both told me how the special effects crew from Backdraft were attached to the project and that several incredible fire sequences had been planned. What is the status of this film?*

JC: I'll make it one day! I promise! You know we

have already spent several million Hong Kong dollars on the film's pre-production. I first had the idea a long time ago, but it wasn't until I saw Ron Howard's Backdraft movie that I knew we could do the special effects I want, but it will be bigger than Backdraft. Then just as we were ready to begin production, ATV (Hong Kong's second major television channel) made a drama series called Flame about Hong Kong firemen, so I put the film on hold. I know that one day I will make it. I like the script and the emotion in the story. I will make it and you, (laughing) you are invited to the set when I make it.

ML: *Thanks. I look forward to accepting your invitation. What about your eastern Western?*

JC: (laughing) This one is coming too!

Johnny To's Lifeline about firemen and Jet Lee's Once Upon A Time in China and America, resulting in a strange release of two variations on two of Jackie's dream projects but neither starring the man himself!)

ML: *Do you ever find it strange that despite you being Jackie Chan and your position in the Hong Kong film industry, you can't always make the films you want to?*

JC: The whole film industry is very very strange! (laughing) I know some of the problems. For my eastern Western the script isn't finalised. And if we make the film, we will have to film it in North America and deal with unions and so many things. I will be using a mainly western cast and crew, and I know they won't work like a Hong Kong crew on a 12-15 hour shift

Even when we were filming Rumble in Canada, the crew were very good but as soon as it's time for lunch, everybody stops exactly at that time, and for the full lunch break!

ML: *I know that for this project, you had Francis Ford Coppolla interested in producing the film, and when myself and action actor Ron Hall (Bloodsport 2, The Slow Die Fast) had a meeting with your friend/manager and business partner Willie Chan in 1993, he told us that it was going to be your next project after Drunken Master 2 and he was quite worried about the fact that you were going to shave your head for the role. What happened?*

JC: (Shrugs shoulders) I don't know! It's going to get made one day though. You know I had the idea for Rumble in the Bronx several years ago. So many times I get ready to do one of these films and something happens and I end up doing a totally different project. (Mike Factoid: While Jackie's long awaited Western, originally titled West West West, has finally gone into production under the name of Shanghai Noon with Jackie's co-stars including Lucy Liu from Payback and Ally McBeal, and Jason Connery son of Sean, Fireman's Story has yet to go into production. What's funny is that at Chinese New Year 1996, the three major movies at the Hong Kong box office were Jackie's Mr. Nice Guy,

and just take twenty minutes for lunch. They have set times for everything, and the cost will be too high if I try to film it like I do in Hong Kong. I won't be able to spend three months on the ending. Even when we were filming Rumble in Canada, the crew were very good but as soon as it's time for lunch, everybody stops exactly at that time, and for the full lunch break! In Hong Kong, the crew will often work and eat at the same time. For this movie I have to make a very good plan and schedule or else I will be in a lot of trouble when we are filming. But wait and see Mike, one day you will get to see all of these movies!

ML: *When I was at your birthday party in April 1994, you and Sammo Hung seemed to reconcile after some years of disagreements. Then at the Hong Kong Film Awards, you, Sammo and Yuen Biao reunited to present a lifetime achievement award to Golden Harvest supremo Raymond Chow, and at the Hong Kong Stuntman's Association Ball a few months ago, the three of you seemed to be getting along fine. As a team, the three of you made some great films together, Project A, Wheels on Meals, Dragons Forever etc.*

And I know that a lot of people, including myself, would very much love to see another triple header from the three of you. What are the chances?

JC: It's going to happen again! Soon! Sammo, Biao and myself, we're more than friends, we are brothers. But when we were all together at Golden Harvest, sometimes I was very involved in my own projects and couldn't always spend time with them. I didn't always have time to work with them, even when I wanted to. So while their faces seem happy when they see me, I think that inside they are angry with me. Then when they both left Golden Harvest, I missed them and try to get the three of us back together again. But, I can't do it all by myself, they have to make the effort too, I can't force them to be my friends again. As I've said, they are my brothers and I love and respect them as such. Now we are talking about working together again, I gave one script to Sammo and he will direct me soon. (Mike Factoid: Sammo and Jackie of course reunited on Thunderbolt with Sammo handling the action for the garage fight and Pachinko parlour, before directing Jackie in Mr. Nice Guy, while Yuen Biao is currently serving as action director on Jackie's Shanghai Noon.)

ML: When I've spoken with your fellow classmate Yuen Wah (Dragons Forever's cigar chomping villain, and Bruce Lee's stunt double for Enter The Dragon) about his lifelong relationship with you, Sammo and Biao. He described it as a brotherhood, that you were a family, and that just like any family, sometimes people disagree and have arguments.

JC: He's right! We're all human; sometimes we get angry at each other but not forever, eventually we start talking again. Yes, we've known each other for so long but that doesn't mean we always want to or have to talk to each other or work together. There is rivalry between us, especially between Sammo and me; we both always want to be the leader. Sammo always treats me like I'm still this little boy at the Opera School when we first met. He is my big brother, and I respect him, I just want him to respect me too!

ML: If you don't mind, can we talk about the man behind the myth: the real Jackie Chan? You're very much a role model and a public figure, a spokesman for Aids Concern, the Royal Hong Kong Police uses your Police Story theme tune for its recruitment ads, you're the tourist ambassador for Hong Kong. Do you find that because you're in the public eye, you have to be that bit more responsible?

JC: You know that I don't ask for any of these things. People observe the way I behave and then ask me to assume these duties. I'm like a goodwill ambassador; the Police call me up and ask me to give some awards, so I do it. Aids Concern asks me to help, I try my best to help. I feel very proud when people refer to me as a role model or think highly of me, so I try harder to be responsible and not let people down.

ML: Jackie, you always seem to be working, either in front of or behind the camera, or doing charity work, or singing, or launching a new product, or giving up your time for interviews with people like me. How do you relax?

JC: Relax! I don't have any free time, so how can I relax! (laughing) My schedule is always full, my secretaries arrange everything for me, and then they give me a timetable. Today, you are interviewing me, and then tomorrow I fly to Taiwan for two days of promotion, then onto Malaysia where I will present two dialysis machines to a hospital, then off to Singapore, then China, then onto Japan for location hunting. I'm very busy, I need a holiday! (laughing)

ML: Jackie, you're held in very high regard by many noted American actors and directors such as Michael Douglas, Oliver Stone and Sylvester Stallone, who not only borrowed the bus stunt from Police Story for Tango & Cash, but also name-checked you in Demolition Man. The rumours relating to the two of you working together are getting stronger and stronger. Will the two of you be teaming up for a forthcoming project?

JC: We hope to. I have been a fan of Sylvester Stallone since the first Rocky movie. I like him because he has worked as an actor, scriptwriter and director, just like me. Also he is very physical and does a lot of his own action, which I like. I feel very happy and honoured to have him as a friend. We're just waiting for the right script to come along, he knows the western market far better than I do. I've said to him that if he finds a script that's good for us, I'll do it, I think we will make a very good team if we work together. (Mike Factoid: Jackie and Sylvester Stallone did team up, however briefly, in Burn Hollywood Burn/An Alan Smithee Film, when they teamed up with Whoopi Goldberg for the ultimate action movie within the movie.)

ML: *A lot of people in the west are trying to catch the flavour of Hong Kong action in their films, with some actors/action directors copying action/stunt scenes directly from*

Hong Kong films. The late Brandon Lee was a very big fan of yours and for the action scenes in Rapid Fire he borrowed heavily from your work in Police Story, the Asian print of The Protector and your last collaboration with Sammo and Biao, Dragons Forever. How do you feel when people re-use your action scenes and stunts for their films?

JC: I feel very happy and very proud. You see when I first started out, I was influenced by a lot of people. I watched a lot of movies by Buster Keaton, Gene Kelly, Harold Lloyd, lots of American stuntmen, to see what they could do and then I'd try and rework their ideas for myself. Now people are turning the tables and copying me, I am happy that my work is good enough for them to want to copy. I feel very flattered.

ML: *I know that you damaged your ankle quite badly during the making of Rumble in the Bronx. What happened?*

JC: It was a pretty easy stunt. (laughing) For some reason, I always seem to get hurt doing the easy stunts! That's what happened when we were filming Armour of God in Yugoslavia, and I fell out of the tree and nearly died. That was also an easy stunt! (laughing) When I'm doing a big stunt I'm more careful, but the stunt in Rumble when I broke two bones was pretty simple. I jumped from a bridge onto the deck of a hovercraft. When I landed, I was falling forward and would have smashed my head on the cabin, so I turned as I landed. But because the whole of the deck is covered with a non-slip material so you don't fall into the water, when I landed and turned, my body and my legs turned, but my ankle didn't! (laughing) Go see the movie, it's much easier to see than for me to talk about it.

ML: *In closing, do you have any messages for your fans worldwide?*

JC: Thank you very much for all of your support and friendship. I am very happy that you like me and I appreciate your support. I hope that you continue to support me and enjoy my films. I hope that we can all meet sometime. Thank you for all your letters and support. Thank you!

PROJECT A

by Matthew Edwards

After the unfair critical mauling and poor box-office receipts of Dragon Lord, Jackie Chan bounced defiantly back with his grand opus Project A, at once distilling new blood into the kung-fu genre by dragging it from the Ching Dynasty into the twentieth century. Brimming with exuberance and verve, Chan demonstrated versatility and willingness towards change, with a feverish tale of a band of ruthless pirates who terrorise the South China Seas.

Joined with his Peking Opera buddies Sammo Hung and Yuen Biao, Project A decimated all the competition with its inextricable fusion of bruising martial arts and slapstick comedy. It also highlighted Chan's love for the silent era of filmmaking with homages to the likes of Charlie Chaplin and Buster Keaton.

Also with the added presence of Sammo Hung, Chan and Hung cleverly orchestrated the action sequences around the plot that in turn drove the movie along, unlike more traditional kung-fu movies that were based loosely around a number of set pieces. Chan's comic imagination reflected an appreciation of a succession of comic geniuses that was woven around awesome and sustained action sequences, that saw Chan progress from a martial arts star into a comedy-action superstar.

Set in Hong Kong during the turn of the century, the film introduces us to Dragon Ma, played by Chan, as a sailor in the coast guards. Decked out in a British tar ice cream suit, we learn of the ongoing feud between the coast guards and the mainland police over the distribution of the force's cash. Dragon's superior argues that his men need better funding if they are to stop the notorious bloodthirsty pirate Sanpao from continuing his wave of violence throughout the South China Seas. However, his rival, Captain Chi, insists the money would be better used on the mainland, claiming Chan's marines are incompetent. Compromising, the Admiral grants the coast guards another chance to stop Sanpao.

mainland police defenceless

Arriving late for duty and de-saddling his bicycle in full motion, Dragon is ordered to get procedure documents signed for the ammunition needed before shipping out. However, it transpires the signature needed is that of Captain Chi who again belittles Dragon and the marines claiming that they would leave the mainland police defenceless with the amount of ammo they were requesting, before declaring that if they were better marksmen they wouldn't need so much ammo. Dragon however gains the last laugh when he quickly places the Captain's glasses on his chair, whereupon he duly sits on them!

Stopping at a local tavern for a farewell bash, we are plunged into the first confrontation between the arrogant mainland police and the coast guards. It is here that we are first introduced to Inspector Tsu, played brilliantly by Yuen Biao. After a bout of verbal insults, two marines retaliate with an offensive remark aimed solely at provoking the police. Here a small fracas erupts, ending with Dragon calming matters down. Apologising, he returns to his marines. However he is tripped in the process, sending him sprawling to the ground. Tzu accuses Dragon of spoiling his clothes and proceeds to pour a tankard of beer over Dragon's head. Dragon gives two options to the disrespectful Tzu, one being to apologise, but before Dragon finishes Tzu declares he has a third, and duly unleashes a kick into Dragon's midriff, sending him once again to the ground. All hell now breaks loose as chairs fly and both factions lay into one another.

Dragon and Tzu square off

In the unfolding chaos one officer is sent crashing into a record player, at once starting it. Dragon and Tzu square off, both dropping their broken bottles and truncheons, before to the first chord of the music they resume fighting.

It is a revelation to see Chan and Biao commencing battle against one another since their "horsebench versus staff" bout two years earlier in The Young Master, especially within such a frenzied and perfectly choreographed scene. Amidst the exhilarating and comical segments of the brawl (watch out for the segment when Chan and Biao both smash a chair over each other's backs, before hiding around a corner and rubbing their backs in agony). Chan and Biao's unquestionable athleticism and grace mesmerise the audience. Chan and Biao show that they are both lithe and agile acrobats, especially when incorporating objects into their stunts. The epitome of this is a scintillating stunt where we witness Chan jumping forward on to a chair that is slung down towards him by Biao. Even more interesting is watching the outtakes at the end of the movie where you realise this stunt took more than one attempt!

This melee ends when the police force arrives, led by Captain Chi. It transpires that Tzu is the nephew of Chi, and he orders the detainment of Dragon and his marines. Dragon's disgruntled superior orders his men's release, claiming Tzu had started the

JC with Sammo Hung at the restaurant brawl in 'Project A'

scuffle in the first place. Repenting, Captain Chi gives orders for their release before the crew assembles in front of the Admiral prior to their departure. However, things go disastrously wrong when their ships are blown up whilst situated in the harbour. As the fire engulfs the night sky, Dragon and his men fear the worst, suspecting foul play from Sanpao's men.

Chou hires petty thief

What transpires, within the confines of a lavish hotel suite, is a deal between wealthy local businessman Chou and Sanpao's henchman who negotiates on his behalf. It becomes apparent that Sanpao has offered protection to Chou's merchant ships in return for information regarding the marines' movements around the coast. He also requests a new deal that sees him obtaining one hundred rifles. Agreeing, Chou hires petty thief Fei, played by Sammo Hung, to steal the rifles with the sole intent of killing him afterwards.

Meanwhile, with their fleet sunk, Dragon and his crew are disbanded and turned into a police unit by Captain Chi, fitted nicely in conical "mollusk" hats.

To make matters worse though, Inspector Tzu is placed in charge, where he revels in putting them through an extremely tough and rigorous training regime.

Their first assigment under Tzu is to arrest Chiang, a wanted gangster who has been hiding in the exclusive V.I.P. club. Just as the police arrive, Sammo is seen leaving the club declaring that he will steal the rifles but only if he himself can hire an accomplice. Spotting Dragon, Sammo hides as the police storm the club demanding Chiang. Dragon locates Chiang and orders his arrest before a fight ensues that ends with Dragon brilliantly locking Chiang up against a wall with a chair. Tzu informs Chiang he is wanted for murder, but Chiang is not prepared to go easily, whereupon he escapes and a scuffle ensues between the police and the club's henchmen.

Dragon, a man who never does things easily, manages to wreck the private club as he tries to apprehend Chiang. The fight sequences here are peppered with dynamite scissors kicks and hard-hitting martial arts, and you can almost feel the bones cracking as they crash on to the marbled floor. Chan himself gets flung down the banister of a flight of stairs. As objects fly, and the elite stuntmen from Hong Kong execute more dangerously painful stunts and flips, Captain Chi arrives. Chi orders Dragon to apologise to Chou, who accuses them of trespass and false accusation, but Dragon quits and proceeds to uncover Chiang by swinging from a chandelier to the balcony above! After a brief duel, Dragon sends Chiang through a stained glass window with a double-footed kick, before he duly unleashes a lethal kick to Chiang's head, sending him tumbling from the balcony towards the floor below. Dragging Chiang to a speechless Captain Chi, Dragon exits rather unhappily.

On his way out Dragon bumps into old pal Fei (Sammo Hung), where he informs Dragon about Sanpao's intentions and his contract to steal the rifles. It transpires they intend to steal the rifles from the police, so Dragon teams up with Fei, who is suspicious of his erratic friend. Emerging from the dark waters tailored in black while sporting traditional opera-style painted faces, Dragon and Fei sneak on to the ship, capturing Captain Chi before proceeding to plunge him into the ocean.

Fei ties a red cloth to the log

Escaping with the rifles they decide to hold them within a log situated on a hillside. Fei ties a red cloth to the log so they can recognise it in the morning. After a brief meeting he takes Sanpao's associates to the bay, only to discover that every log now has a red cloth nailed on it. Suspicious of being double-crossed, they turn on Fei, just as Dragon's old superior arrives, who himself has been tipped off by Dragon as to the whereabouts of the rifles.

Fei flees to Dragon's place, but is ultimately followed. Amidst accusations of betrayal they both

forget their differences and team up together, engaging in more fighting, before both are captured at gunpoint. Attempting to extract the whereabouts of the rifles, Fei whips the gun away from the captor's hands. In tandem they demolish the inept attempts of the villains, at once sending them plummeting into tables and walls. After a brief chase, his assailants pursue on bicycles! As Dragon escapes he unfortunately collides with his old boss, Captain Chi, who takes great delight in detaining him. However, Dragon gives Chi the slip when he handcuffs him to another officer.

ingeniously handled

Escaping into the back streets, here we are launched into an exquisite scene clearly influenced by Buster Keaton. This has to be one of Chan's most over the top and ingeniously handled sequences in any of his movies. With the tight narrow streets resembling some kind of maze, Dragon, taking off on Chi's bicycle, is chased not only by Chou's men, but also the police!

His love for the silent movie era is clearly in evidence here, as Chan uses ladders and Dutch doors in the same way as Chaplin. As one attacker closes in he rides past a Dutch door and proceeds to knock on the top half. The unsuspecting occupant opens it just in time to smack the attacker in the face! Another move worth mentioning is when Chan uses his bicycle as a weapon, although this really has to be seen to be believed.

Dangling precariously on the small wooden roof

Demobilising others with a pole used like an Old English lance, Dragon rides into a small tea-room where Fei is hiding. Unable to stop, he crashes through the tea-room's barriers, but is fortunately caught just in time by Fei. While Dragon is dangling precariously on the small wooden roof, his pursuers storm the building, but only manage to ride off the roof onto the hard ground below. Again, Hong Kong's elite perform stunts that look like they really hurt and begs the question - surely there must be easier work around in Hong Kong?

As Fei and Dragon bicker (that's all they seem to do earlier on in this film), the rest of the gang show up intent on retrieving the valuable rifles. Facing

up to their attackers, they beat them into submission. After becoming recaptured by Chi and handcuffed to a flagpole, he proceeds to combat his foes before climbing the flagpole and jumping through the window of a clock tower. By now your adrenaline is really pumping, but Dragon has no plans of relenting now and pulls off his trump card in this quite exhilarating scene.

Using the clock's gears to create a mini duel with one of the arms smugglers, he then climbs out onto the clock's face in a truly daredevil stunt. Holding on to one of the clock's hands, one of the smugglers opens up the face to leave poor old Dragon dangling in suspended animation. Aiming a gun at Dragon, it all seems over until Tzu arrives and shoots the smuggler in the head.

So ends this perfectly placed action sequence

Too tired to hang on, Chan falls in movie-like slow-motion through two awnings and hits the ground hard! Not content with one shot of this remarkable stunt, we are presented with all kinds of angles, which seem to differ each time! I would say he must have shot this scene at least three times, because every take seems to be different, especially the outtake at the end of the film! So ends this perfectly placed action sequence, unless like me, you rewound the tape and watched it again, your brain not quite comprehending the event you had just witnessed.

Obviously the pirates have no sense of fun because none of this impresses them, and by now they have become completely neurotic about getting those rifles. Enraged, they decide to shanghai a ship full of foreign dignitaries and hold them to ransom. This, interestingly enough, is the first action scene played out on the ocean. After the pirates have run amok, we are introduced to the now infamous Sanpao and his reign of terror.

Dragon uncovers a shady deal between Chou and his Admiral, accusing his officer of helping a known criminal. Consumed with guilt he repents. This in turn leads to the reformation of the coast guards, and the implementation of Project A.

Dragon proceeds to kidnap Chou, where he extracts the whereabouts of Sanpao with a violent and numbing beating. Then impersonating Chou, he is escorted to Sanpao's secret hideout, followed closely by Tzu and his men.

slow-motion shots

Once inside Sanpao's liar, Dragon is made guest of honour at Sanpao's birthday celebrations. Discreetly creeping off, Dragon, with the help of Fei, rescues the hostages, before Dragon, Tzu and Fei team up for the accustomed end battle. With Sanpao's fleet now blown sky high and Dragon uncovered as a fraud, all manner of scuffles erupt, as our heroes must defeat Sanpao and his henchmen. Tzu, accompanied by one of his men, begins firing at Sanpao's forces, before some nicely executed slow-motion shots display Tzu pulverising his opponents with some acrobatic kicks.

Using grenades, they seal off the entrance in order to stop Sanpao's reinforcements from entering. By now it is four against one as Dragon and company lead an onslaught against the weary Sanpao. After a swashbuckling duel between Dragon and Sanpao, the demon-pirate is finally beaten in one of the most stylish deaths caught on celluloid, that ranks alongside Andy Lau's suicide in Eric Tsang's The Tigers. Rolling Sanpao up in a carpet, they stick a grenade inside, leaving Sanpao to scatter himself over a wide area as our heroes jump to safety.

With our heroes stranded, they must find their way back to the mainland by raft. However, it seems their geography and navigation skills are not on a par with their martial arts!

Jackie Chan has again cemented his image as Asia's number one star, and Project A is believed by many to be his best work yet. His winning formula of transporting kung-fu into a more modern era and the inclusion of Sammo Hung and Yuen Biao ensures that it is only a matter of time before Hollywood comes around knocking.

GEN-X COPS

A THOMAS CHUNG & WILLIE CHAN PRODUCTION

Reviewed by Mike Leeder

Hong Kong 1999, a sinister alliance has been formed between a faction of the Hong Kong Triads and members of the Japanese Yakuza. When a shipment of lethal explosives goes missing, veteran Hong Kong Police officer Eric Tsang forms a team of offbeat young policemen to track it down. These three Gen-X Cops are Jack (Nicholas Tse), Match (Stephen Fung) and Alien (Sam Lee), assisted by the lovely computer genius Y-2K (Grace Yip). They find themselves up against a similarly youthful gang boss, Daniel (Dan Wu), and the shadowy Japanese mastermind behind him, Tiger (Toru Nakamura). Throw in rival Triad boss Francis Ng, the return of Match's long lost love Jayme, now Daniel's girlfriend, and a condescending Police Superintendent (Moses Chan), and turn of the century Hong Kong becomes a stunning backdrop for this showdown between the law and the lawless, with Hong Kong's Convention Centre as the location for the final showdown.

Hong Kong Action Cinema enters a new era with Gen-X Cops, the first co-production between Jackie Chan's JC Group and Media Asia. A hot young cast, Nicholas Tse, Stephen Fung, Sam Lee, Grace Yip, Daniel Wu etc, and strong director Benny Chan are teamed with Oscar winning special effects expert Joe Viskocil (Apollo 13, Independence Day) to provide the film with a truly explosive finale, while Hong Kong vehicular action maestro Bruce Law handles the car stunts, and none other than Nicky Li and the Jackie Chan Stuntmen's Club provide the physical action. Veterans of several James Bond movies handle the film's parachuting action. Throw in master cinematographer Arthur Wong, whose credits include Crime Story, Once Upon A Time In China, Knock Off and many more, and a brief but genuinely funny cameo appearance by a certain Jackie Chan and you have one of the most enjoyable Hong Kong movies of the last few years.

Directed by Benny Chan, whose skillful hands have helmed such classics as A Moment of Romance, The Big Bullet and Who Am I?, the film belts along at a breakneck pace. It's not a perfect film, but it's still one hell of an enjoyable ride. The cast is led by actor and singer Nicholas Tse (son of 60s idol Patrick Tse), who made his acting debut in Andrew Lau's Young & Dangerous: The Prequel. The young Tse threw himself into this role big time, and gets the chance to show that not only can he act but the boy can move. He handles the physicality of the role very well, proving adept in the fight scenes, performing a lot of his own stunts and in true Jackie Chan fashion suffered for his art when a stunt went wrong during the films finale and he was slammed shin first into a gantry 50 feet up. Give the man a few more years and more strong roles and Nicholas Tse could well be the new Hong Kong action star.

Stephen Fung, who until recently had been known more for his arty roles in such films as Bishonen and The Poet, sadly doesn't come across as well. He handles the action OK, even taking on my old buddy Brad Allan in a fight scene that while appearing in the trailer and the lobby cards was for some reason cut from the finished film, but his performance isn't appealing. He doesn't come across in any way as a likeable character. Sam Lee from Made in Hong Kong pretty much steals the show in the hero department. Not only does he give the best performance of the three acting wise, but his eccentricities also fit the role of Alien perfectly, you could really imagine that he comes from a galaxy far, far away. He also throws himself into the action very well. He's not the most graceful or best looking fighter, far from it, but the way he fights, the way he acts, it'll keep you laughing. I especially enjoyed his brief fight scene with Japanese action actor Keiji Sato from Hitman. The lovely Grace Yip is incredibly cute as Y-2K, and handles herself well in her brief acting and action sequences, but her roles in this film and in A Man Called Hero call for her to do very little beyond turn up, look cute, perform a few brief moves and that's it, although she does do it very well. The girl is cute, gutsy and looks like she can really move, give her a chance someone!

JC Group's own Daniel Wu really impressed me in this film. He came to Hong Kong a few years back to pursue a career as an action actor, but has found himself mainly headlining some intense dramas,

at redemption and finally making the grade. Francis Ng makes the most of his brief role as Daniel's Triad rival, with a speech by Bey Logan that's so cool, if unprintable, that I'm going to have to rip it off, I mean pay homage to it in a future production: "Last night, I had a dream…" Japanese actor Toru Nakamura, who some of you may have seen in Blue Tiger with Virginia Madsen (if you haven't seen it, check it out!), and New York City Cop which saw him teamed with Mira Sorvino and Conan Lee (if you haven't seen this, thank the lord!), steals the show acting wise. He brings such great presence and charisma to his role as Tiger the Yakuza boss. From his most minute mannerisms to his admirable martial arts skills and his way cool dress sense, you know he's a baddy from the moment you see him, but he's a great one.

The supporting cast all do their best, with the only drawback being that so much of Brad Allan's work on the movie was cut - he turns up, you keep expecting him to fight, but he never does, instead

I'd previously seen a clip in the trailer where he came across as a whiny little kid and it had put me off of him immediately.

Bishonen and City Of Glass to name but two, before making a transition into action movies. I'd previously seen a clip in the trailer where he came across as a whiny little kid and it had put me off him immediately. However upon watching the whole film, I realized that was what he was trying to put across. His character in the film is struggling to prove that he can run the Triad group when all he really is, is just a kid, ready to follow anyone who'll promise him a better deal. Strangely enough, of the leads, Daniel is probably the most talented martial arts wise but doesn't get to throw a punch or kick in the movie; instead he gets to swagger with a mean Uzi 9mm. (Look for Daniel to headline the next Media Asia/JC Group release Purple Storm, co-starring Joan Chen and directed by old friend Teddy Chen from Downtown Torpedoes.) Eric Tsang provides the laughs as the Gen-X Cops' put upon boss. He's looked down upon by his fellow officers and sees solving this case as his one chance

handling all manner of stuntwork including doubling for Eric Tsang in the fat suit. Numerous members of the Friday Lunch Club make appearances in the movie too: Wing Chun maestro Chris Collins, Hung Gar's David Taylor and Mark "the Drunken Master" Holland, and Hung Gar stylist David Leong, soon to be seen in Treasure Hunters. And a special award should go to Media Asia's man for all seasons Bey Logan. As the SWAT Team Commander he only gets a few lines but he makes the most of them, and I look forward to seeing his return in all future Media Asia productions. Keiji Saito, the Japanese crimelord from Jet Li's Hitman, also makes the most of his limited screentime when he demolishes Sam Lee in Hot Gossip disco. Maybe it's just me but, while I really enjoyed the movie, I wanted more in the way of physical action. Yes, the film's parachuting scenes are quite impressive and pretty well handled, and the films explosive finale is good, but I wanted

more in the way of martial arts. Hmm... maybe in Gen-X Cops 2. As for Jackie's cameo, it's a worthy one that always catches the audience and it works a hell of a lot better than the one in Project S.

Gen-X Cops received as much hype and press attention here as Star Wars: The Phantom Menace did overseas, complete with various trailers, early promo posters, making ofs etc, and while I wasn't expecting it to, it pretty much lived up to the hype. Yes, it's not perfect and there are a few scenes that should be changed and I think that more of the film's physical action should have been left in, but it's still one of the most enjoyable Hong Kong movies in a long time. So while you're waiting for the next Jackie film, I can't think of many better ways of passing the time than by sitting back and watching Gen-X Cops. It's fun, it's funky, and wait till you see the DVD of it that they're gonna put out!

Thanks to Bey Logan and Media Asia for the pictures accompanying this review.

GEN-X COPS DVD

review by Albert Valentin

Directed by acclaimed director Benny Chan Muksing, the film stars Nicholas Tse (Young & Dangerous: The Prequel), Sam Lee, Stephen Fung, Daniel Wu (Purple Storm, 2000 AD), Toru Nakayama (New York Cop), and Grace Yip, in a story of crime and how four people that you would never expect to stop the bad guys, do just that. Anyway, I came across some great extras on the DVD edition of the film. The DVD edition includes some deleted scenes, a behind the scenes look at the film, talent files, and theatrical trailers.

TALENT FILES

The only talent file available on the US DVD edition of the film is that of the main man himself, Jackie Chan, whose Jackie Chan Group presented the film along with Media Asia. His talent file consists of his biography and his achievements of winning Hong Kong Film Awards for action choreography for the films Rumble in the Bronx and Who Am I? The talent file also includes the listing of Jackie's autobiography.

THEATRICAL TRAILERS

The DVD contains the theatrical trailers of two films, Gen-X Cops and Jackie Chan's Who Am I? The trailer for Gen X-Cops shows close-ups of the film's stars and various action sequences. The trailer also includes specialized logos for the characters of Jack, Alien, Match, and Y-2K.

The trailer for Jackie Chan's Who Am I? begins with the opening sequences: where the information of the energy source is stolen and how it is up to Jackie to get it back, despite losing all his memory. Do not really expect much from the Who Am I? trailer, but the Gen-X Cops trailer is a great one, as it will make you want to watch the film.

GEN-X COPS: NO PAIN, NO GAIN!

The highlight of the DVD Special Features is the making of the film. This behind the scenes look at the film includes interviews with cast members Nicholas Tse (Jack), Sam Lee (Alien), Stephen Fung (Match), Daniel Wu (Daniel), as well as director/writer/producer Benny Chan.

Gen-X Cops: No Pain, No Gain! begins with the explanation of the term "Generation-X". Star Daniel Wu describes it as rebelling, "doing what you want". The film also has a shot of a party that took place after principle photography was completed. Jackie said that after seeing a rough cut of the film, he was impressed by the fighting skills of Nicholas Tse, who he described as "fighting like a young Jackie Chan".

This comment leads to Nicholas talking about how he likes doing his own stunts, especially for this film. He explains that his most dangerous stunt was escaping from a burning pool. He feared he was willing to give it a try, despite the risk of being seriously burned.

From there, director Benny Chan explained how he was warned by friends of his not to use newcomers for the film because they would "drive him mad". At first, Benny said he didn't have a problem, but sooner or later, the stars did, in fact,

Stars on the run! Nicholas Tse, Stephen Fung and Sam Lee

"drive him mad". The cast members said that Benny was like a "big kid" on the set of the film. During breaks, the cast would goof around on set, but Benny didn't care. According to Tse and Lee, Benny Chan didn't do anything to restrain their performance.

One of the most dangerous stunts of the film was when stars Nicholas Tse, Stephen Fung, and Sam Lee had to run out of a warehouse that would explode. After taking a few practice runs, the three stars were ready for the big stunt. They knew it was a one-take shot and that it had to be done right. The actors gave their views on the dangerous stunt. Sam Lee was happy that the stunt was completed.

From there, the three main cast members began talking about themselves. First, it was Stephen Fung, who played Match. He is described as easy-going with a low profile. He flirts with the girls. Basically, Match's persona is similar to the real life persona of Stephen Fung. According to Sam Lee, Nicholas's character of Jack is described as cool and opinionated. According to Lee, when Nicholas matures, he will be better in both acting and fighting. Well, Sam Lee's character of Alien is exactly like Sam himself. Alien is described as a unique, outstanding person. Sam describes himself as an irresponsible and wild guy. Nicholas said that acting like Alien is the Sam Lee way of acting.

The feature then describes the stunts used, including aerial stunts courtesy of Tom Saunders, martial arts and gunplay courtesy of longtime Jackie Chan stunt team member Li Chung-chi, as well as the visual effects. The visual effects, specifically the blowing up of the Hong Kong Convention Center, was done by Jon Viskocil, the man responsible for the White House explosion in the Hollywood blockbuster Independence Day, as well as for his work on Godzilla and Star Wars, with help from visual effects supervisor Sam Nicholson. According to Nicholson, Gen-X Cops is the first Hong Kong film to use the special effects that were used in films such as Independence Day.

Then the fans are treated to a music video of a song titled "You Can't Stop Me", sung by the film's three main stars, Nicholas Tse, Sam Lee, and Stephen Fung. The music video includes scenes from the film and the performers in the recording studio.

DELETED SCENES

The DVD edition of the film also includes scenes that were cut out from the film's release. They include the following scenes:

*   During police training, Jack is lying around while Alien is practicing his sharp shooting skills. Meanwhile, Match breaks into Commander Lo's apartment and safe, discovering money that was given to Lo by three students. When Jack is confronted by the three students for lying around, Lo arrives and confronts Jack, only to find out Match has discovered the truth about how Lo was bribed by the three students into passing a test.

*   Inspector Chan (played by Eric Tsang) brings the team of Jack, Alien, and Match to his apartment, which becomes the team's headquarters, and they are forced to fill out insurance forms.

*   The team is introduced to Y-2K (played by Grace Yip), who is out for revenge against the men who killed her brother. A fight ensues when Alien insults Y-2K, and then Match and Alien begin to fight each other too.

*   The boys are sent to a club, courtesy of Daniel (played by Daniel Wu), in order to kill crime lord Lok. After a long conversation, Lok discovers that Jack is working for Daniel and it becomes a double cross as Tooth (Terence Yip, of Hot War) confronts Daniel and double-crosses him.

*   When the boys and Daniel return to shore after a narrow escape from Lok and his crew, Alien shows aggression towards Daniel and attempts to confront Daniel, despite Jack's plea to Alien that Daniel is the only connection towards Akatora. As Alien attempts to hit Daniel with a two-by-four, Daniel points a gun towards all three men.

There is so much to see, but only if you get the DVD edition of the United States release of Gen-X Cops, courtesy of Columbia-TriStar Home Video. Not only will you get to enjoy the film - you will get to check out some of these fantastic special features.

Factoids:

Gen-Y Cops, the sequel to Gen-X Cops, completed filming recently and is scheduled for a Christmas 2000 release throughout Asia. For the sequel Jackie Chan and Media Asia joined forces with Regent Films from America. The sequel sees the return of original Gen-Xers Stephen Fung and Sam Lee, along with a whole bunch of new faces, including Edison Chen and Maggie Q newly signed to The JC Group, Richard Sun from Bride With White Hair 2, and Coola Girl Rachel Ngan. It also stars Christy Chung, Paul Rudd, Mark Hicks, and Reuben Langdon. Plus the film sees the return of Ron "I do special kicks! Where's the cheese?" Smoorenburg.

Would you buy a second-hand car from this man? Daniel Wu in 'Gen-X Cops'

DANIEL WU

The Next Generation of Hong Kong Action Movie Players

Screen Power Editor Richard Cooper attends the World Premiere of Jackie Chan's and Media Asia's latest movie collaboration, the action thriller "Purple Storm", in the heart of London's Leicester Square.

Wednesday 13th October 1999, and I am standing outside London's Warner West End Theatre. A huge billboard above me advertises the movie I'm invited here to see. The film in question is "Purple Storm", an action thriller starring one of Hong Kong's brightest new talents, Daniel Wu.

Upon my arrival, and before a scheduled celebratory Lion Dance troupe kicks off the late

morning's activities, I exchange a few pleasantries with the guy who's invited me here - friend, and Media Asia exec Bey Logan. Before long, Bey is dragging me around the gathered crowd of people, who I assume are an assortment of fans, press, and V.I.P. guests, and introduces me to the guy all this fanfare is put on for - Daniel Wu.

Daniel Wu is a guy who will be among the new

breed of Hong Kong cinema players. Quite a responsibility, but he's confident things will work out okay because not only has he already starred in one of Hong Kong's biggest summer blockbusters, "Gen-X Cops", but he's also managed by one of the, if not the, best people in Asian artiste representation, the famous Willie Chan, my good friend, and manager of the world's number one action superstar, Jackie Chan.

As I later witness after watching "Purple Storm", on-screen Daniel's flipping and kicking and oozing with such charisma, confidence and loudness, while off-screen he's more reserved but extremely funny, and one hell of a nice guy, as I found out after a bit to eat and a drink in a quaint little restaurant in London's China Town where we conducted the following exclusive interview:

Richard Cooper:

   Dan, first of all, welcome to the UK.

Daniel Wu:

   Hi...

RC: Is this your first time in England?

DW: It's like my fifth I think, so far...

RC: Fifth?

DW: Right. I've got a brother-in-law here, so I come back.

RC: You were raised in the States, so when did you first come to Hong Kong?

DW: The first time was... '97. I graduated from University and went out for the... Well, I've been back many times as a child because my mom grew up there, and I have close relatives over there. So I used to go back every summer, and then '97 was special because of the Handover, so I wanted to be there for this historical moment.

RC: Have you always been interested in movies?

DW: No, not really. I mean I always have been sort of like a fan of movies. I always watched Hong Kong movies, and because I've been doing martial arts my whole life it was definitely an interest to watch Jackie, and Jet Li, and all those kind of people.

RC: Now, for the readers who don't know - you are represented by the famous Willie Chan of The JC Group. Willie himself is a very famous and well respected movie producer in Hong

Daniel in a scene from '2000 AD'

Kong, and one of the best in artiste management. How did you get to be represented by him?

DW: That was really interesting because it was actually through Jackie. I have always been a big fan of Jackie's of course, and I had the opportunity to meet him at a party, and then the next minute we're talking about going to see Willie. I mean we barely met, (laughing) I was like, "Why do you want me to meet Willie?" He said, "Oh, you know, you have a good look, and I know you can fight." So I met Willie, and the next day I met Jackie again, and he tested me out and that kind of stuff, and it went on from there.

RC: *So what is your martial arts background? What have you studied?*

DW: I studied Shaolin kung-fu for five years, when I was very young.

RC: *What age were you when you started training in Shaolin?*

that close tie that way because it was the same style.

RC: *Being associated with Jackie's company, do you train with him? Or Ken Low and the stunt team?*

DW: (short pause) Um... not so much. A little bit here and there. I mean we go just to keep in shape. I remember when I first came in and said, "Come on, let's go and train." And they were like, "No man, we're tired from filming!" (laughing) I guess when you've had more experience, your training time is more precious to you. So when I get a chance with them, I'll look forward to that.

RC: *Didn't you shoot a commercial with Jackie and Ken Low?*

DW: Oh yeah, a long time ago. Actually that was when I'd just signed on with The JC Group. I had gotten my first film but I hadn't started filming yet. So they wanted me to go with them to China to see what it was like filming. So I

I was kind of a hyperactive child anyway, right. So they wouldn't let me learn until I was about ten when I had calmed down a little bit.

DW: Ten. What happened was when I was five or six, "Shaolin Temple" came out in the United States, 1980. And it was the first time I saw real kung-fu on the screen, because my parents took me to China Town to go see the movie. From that day I was like, "I gotta learn it, I gotta learn it!" And finally... I was kind of a hyperactive child anyway, right. So they wouldn't let me learn until I was about ten when I had calmed down a little bit. (laughing)

RC: *So Jackie has been one of your major influences in the martial arts...*

DW: Definitely, definitely.

RC: *Who else apart from Jackie ?*

DW: Jet Lee of course, but basically those two. Because I later went on to study Wushu. You know about Wushu?

RC: *Yeah.*

DW: Because my teacher had grown up with Jet Lee, and the Beijing Wushu Team, so you had

went along but I didn't know I was going to be in the commercial until Jackie goes, "Hey, come on!" (laughing)

RC: *(laughing) He surprised you?*

DW: Yeah. So I'm running alongside him, and it was multiple shots of him running through this city, and as each shot goes on, there's more and more people. So me and Ken are the original two, Ken's on the left, and I'm on the right, and Jackie's in the middle, and the group gets bigger, and in the end there's a hundred and some people. Lot of fun.

RC: *Earlier on this morning we watched your new movie "Purple Storm".*

DW: Right.

RC: *We were very impressed. The special effects were great.*

DW: Cool. I'm glad you liked it.

RC: *So for the readers who won't have a chance to see the movie yet for a few months...*

DW: Actually, not until the end of November.

RC: *A November release. So what's the story about? And what can people expect from it?*

DW: (Short pause) The story is basically about a good and evil kind of thing. It's about my character. He loses his memory. He's originally a bad guy, a terrorist. And he's got a very good relationship with his boss, his Sifu almost, and he loses his memory. Then the police decide that maybe they could trick him and say that he was a good guy, and all along he was an undercover cop. He believes it, because he doesn't know anything else about himself at that point. So they send him back in with his boss, and my character, he thinks that he is an undercover cop, but all of a sudden he starts having these flashbacks remembering things. His memory is coming back, right. So then he becomes confused because he has two images in his mind. Images that they planted in, and images of his real life childhood, and the killing and all the things he had done before. So he's really confused, and there's a part where he's schizophrenic, where he really is not sure who he really is. And the more climactic part is when he realises who he was, and what he can be. You know, like "What do you choose?" You know, if you've got a chance to start over, "What do you choose?" It's an interesting plot...

you said, all the planes cruising by, that was really good. I'm not sure if it's a trend, I think it's a trend in the bigger budget films, because I think Hong Kong is also very good at being able not to do special effects, like what Jackie has been doing all these years. I think when they have the budget and have some idea to make a film better with the special effects, I think they'll use it more. And now we're seeing that there are companies in Hong Kong doing the computer graphics, and I think they'll use it as an opportunity to enhance a film, rather than like in Hollywood where they will rely on it in a film. Like say "Independece Day", that's what the film is about, right, or like "Godzilla", it's about special effects. But these films are about... kind of like your basic Hong Kong film but with this new layer on top. I find it interesting.

RC: *"Gen-X Cops", produced by Jackie's company and Media Asia and directed by Chan Muk-sing of "Who Am I?" fame was a big success at this year's Hong Kong box-office. What can people in the West expect from this one?*

DW: I think it was a great hit because it was such a new fresh idea, and one where there were all these new young guys, teenagers. If you think about it, there's a big gap between the stars from before, like in the late 80s and early 90s, to the people now. I mean there's a ten year

Because the first day I met Jackie I realised how much of a caring person he is. You know that anyway, right. But, he cares not only just about people, but the things he's involved in too.

RC: *As I said before, the special effects are very impressive. Do you think it's a current trend now that Hong Kong movies are starting to put special effects in? The airport scene near the end of the movie was amazing, with all those planes.*

DW: Right, yeah. I was pretty surprised too because this is the first time I've seen this cut with the special effects. And I almost didn't notice them at first. I was like, "Wait a second I don't remember that being there!" (laughing) Like

age difference, and what happened was there was nothing inbetween, because those guys before had the market. I wouldn't say in control, but they were the stars. Now it's getting to the point where they don't want to do action movies anymore. So it's like, "Okay, we need these new guys." So, the excitement about it was let's see what these new guys are going to do, added on top with the special effects. This is the first time we've had a Hollywood company make special effects for a Hong Kong film. You know the Hong Kong Convention Centre?

Serious drama in 'Purple Storm' - Daniel with veteran actress Joan Chen

RC: *Yeah.*

DW: You see the Convention Centre explode, and these things, and it's really exhilarating and exciting, and it adds to the flavour of the film. The film is really your typical Hong Kong fast-paced action, and so when you add all those new things it becomes this really new fresh apple if you like.

RC: *Over the last few years Hong Kong movies have, due to a number of reasons, been on a downward trend. Nowadays, Jackie and his company is helping the Hong Kong Film Industry by inspiring and recruiting new up and coming talents like yourself. What do you think about this?*

DW: I think it's really good. Because the first day I met Jackie I realised how much of a caring person he is. You know that anyway, right. But, he cares not only just about people, but the things he's involved in too. So, to him it's really important that the Hong Kong Film Industry keeps going. You know, because he was such a really important part, and still is such a really important part of Hong Kong film history at a time when it was the golden peak time, and he was the king, still like today. So, it's really important to him that he keeps going. He can't be irresponsible and say, "Oh, I'm retiring now, screw it!" you know. But he's like, "No, we can't do this, this is part of our culture. Part of the Hong Kong culture is filming. And so we can't just let it die. Just because I'm not going to be making as many films anymore doesn't mean I don't have the responsibility." But, I think that's the great thing about Jackie, he does care.

RC: *Do you think Jackie will still carry on a few years yet making films?*

DW: Oh yeah. For sure. I think especially because he's still on top. The number one. And also now, of course, he's in Hollywood doing these big Hollywood films which I know has always been a dream of his. He's definitely still on the up and up.

RC: *Your first few movies were serious dramas, then you did "Young & Dangerous: The Prequel", then "Gen-X Cops" and now "Purple Storm".*

DW: That's Right.

RC: *What's this new film you're currently making for Media Asia? "Y-2K" is it?*

DW: Yeah, "Y-2K" which is now called "2000 AD".

RC: *What's this one about, then?*

DW: It's kind of a conspiracy thriller action film all in one. It's about a couple of very typical Hong Kong young guys who are in to computers. But, I think it's very typical of a global thing happening now with a lot of young kids these days, they are very good at computers, and playing virtual games, and maybe learning martial arts. But what happens when you put these guys in a real situation? Can they handle it? I mean you can learn martial arts for so many years, but if you get put in a war or something it's totally different. Or you're put into a situation where you really have to fight somebody for your life, or let's say even a competition, something like that. So these guys are very good at war games, and playing virtual flying games, and things like that, they are experts in that. But it's all a glassed-over reality. Then they get involved in a very big conspiracy involving Aaron Kwok, who is also in the film. His brother gets killed, and we get pulled into this real life conspiracy, and all of a sudden this is not a game, this is real life. You know, how do we react? And I think it's really kind of interesting at that point, this reality, this virtual reality even, these young guys getting their butts kicked around the place (laughing) and then having to realise, "Hey, what can we use from our knowledge of virtual stuff to survive?"

RC: *It does sound very interesting. Good luck with that project. How do you find fighting on screen? I remember asking Jackie this question on the set of "Who Am I?" in Rotterdam and his reply was, "Acting is much easier!" (laughing)*

DW: (laughing) Yeah of course, I think what's most difficult is like in "Purple Storm" for instance, I'm doing a whole lot of heavy action, and then all of a sudden doing drama, then going back to heavy action again. It's difficult flipping back around. It's just two completely different things. One is expression of your emotions and feelings, and the other is an expression of your body and your art form, of whatever it is. I like it personally, because you know I've been watching kung-fu movies all my life, and then learning martial arts. So it's good. It's kind of like coming around full circle. But it's totally different doing movie martial arts than real life martial arts.

RC: *Let's say in ten years time or sooner, you get a break in Hollywood. Would you like to make the transition like Jackie has and have the luxury to make movies in both the East and the West?*

DW: Yeah, it's a question that gets asked a lot. And I'd have to say that if it's a good opportunity... because you know what, I really can't stand the stereotypical Hollywood view of Asians. Every time you have an Asian guy in a film it's like they play this oriental music and they're in China Town. You know, things like that. And I think that it's not truly representative because I grew up in the States, and I know there are millions of other people who didn't grow up in China Town or didn't grow up in that environment, and it doesn't relate. You look at it and you say, if you are an Asian American watching, "That's not me!" That's like saying all African Americans like to Rap! It's not true. I don't want to break into that kind of market if it's going to be that way!

RC: *Good point.*

DW: Yeah, so I much prefer being home in Hong Kong. Doing films that make me happy, and make a lot of sense to me artistically and creatively speaking, rather than doing something very kind of cheesey - Hollywood style. So it depends on things like that.

RC: *Just like Jackie waited for the right script after "The Protector" before he went back to Hollywood for "Rush Hour".*

DW: Right, exactly, because he realised after "The Protector" that this wasn't the kind of thing he wanted. It wasn't the kind of image he wanted to create. So, no, I don't need that. I'll wait, and see if anything good comes along, but I'm not in a rush. Although, I think it's very important to have some Asian American actors and actresses out there in Hollywood.

RC: *You are a young guy anyway - how old are you actually?*

DW: I'm Twenty-five.

RC: *That is young, and I'm not just saying that because I'm also twenty-five... (laughing) What's going to happen after your new movie, "2000 AD"? Are there any other movie projects in the pipeline?*

DW: Yeah, we're all talking about "Downtown Torpedoes 2" with Teddy Chen again.

RC: *Teddy who directed "Purple Storm"?*

DW: Right. Also there's another Stanley Kwan movie, a drama - back to drama again. And some other projects, sort of like in flow right now.

RC: *You had a cameo in "Gorgeous" didn't you?*

DW: (laughing) Right, right.

RC: *What scene are you in so people can look out for you?*

DW: There's a scene... it's like a one-shot. The director Vincent Kok is a friend of mine. He said, "Hey, come on, come out today, it will be on a boat, it's a nice day." So we went out there. I play a photographer's assistant. It's me and Stephen Fung from "Gen-X", he plays the photographer, and Ken Wong from "Downtown Torpedoes". So the three of us are playing photographers. And they had models on the boat and everything. (laughing)

RC: *Sounds a tough job! (laughing)*

DW: Yeah, it was. (laughing)

RC: *So apart from your own movies, can we expect to see you in a few cameo roles in Jackie's movies? You're not a background cowboy in "Shanghai Noon" then? (laughing)*

DW: (laughing) Not as of yet! But, we'll see...

RC: *Dan, thanks a lot for your time, congratulations on "Purple Storm" and I hope to see you next time I'm in Hong Kong.*

DW: Hey, no problem. Yeah, cool, see you when you next come to Hong Kong.

At the Hong Kong Premiere of 'Purple Storm'

OPERATION CONDOR
Armour of God II

By Matthew Edwards

Billed at the time as the biggest martial arts epic ever made, Jackie reprised his role as "The Asian Hawk" (though he's called "Condor" in this sequel), the Asian equivalent of Indiana Jones, five years after the original "Armour of God". Whereas "Armour of God" was a brilliant addition to Jackie's resume, the film became best remembered as the one that nearly killed Jackie after he plummeted twenty feet when a relatively simple stunt went horribly wrong...

Not deterred, and spurred on by the fact that Armour of God became one of his highest grossing films, Jackie sensed a niche in the "Condor" franchise that he could exploit. Determined to construct a film of grand proportions and to equal that of Hollywood movies, Operation Condor eclipsed the original in terms of scale and scope with its lavish production values and stunning cinematography. It is also one of the few sequels to garner the prestige of being better than its predecessor.

Shot on location in Barcelona and the Sahara Desert, with an original budget of 80,000,000 Hong Kong dollars, the film quickly spiralled out of control with problems in the shooting schedule, personnel and budget. However, this is thankfully belied by the final film, as the spectacular action set-pieces set another precedent that Jackie would again have to surpass. The film also boasts a rich vein of humour that from its absurd beginning sets the tone for the rest of the movie.

group of mysterious natives

Clearly taking Raiders of the Lost Ark's opening as inspiration, Operation Condor begins in a not too dissimilar fashion as Jackie goes searching for archaeological treasures. In what seems like the final reel of some lost Jackie classic, our man Chan (Condor) is first seen power gliding over a set of remote Amazon islands before landing on a hillside. Abseiling down into the confines of a small cave, Condor wanders into a cavern governed by a group of mysterious natives who worship a strange demonic statue. Surrounding the statue is a set of glowing green crystals, and despite his best attempts at being discreet when taking them, Condor's efforts evidently lean more towards the conspicuous.

Trying not to arouse the wrath of the natives, Condor tries to appease them with a little friendly banter. Oddly though, the natives seem more than happy for Jackie to pilfer their crystals and it's only when Jackie takes some of their holy water that they turn on him. Suddenly lots more natives appear, congregating inside the cavern where he is informed of the dreadful fate that awaits those who drink the sacred water: they must marry the fat ugly native leader!

Obviously Condor would rather die than live a life of torment and quickly flees, whereupon needless to say the enraged natives pursue him. After Condor discharges a flare into one hapless bunch he escapes outside and hides in the cascades of foliage. Scaring one native with a tiger photo, Jackie jumps inside a huge transparent inflatable bubble that is reminiscent of a hamster's exercise ball. Here Jackie makes his escape as he bounces down hillsides and upon certain native members! Finally he bounces down a sheer vertical drop on one of the island's cliff faces, only to discover that he has lost all of his crystals.

The final phase of this excellent prologue is completed when Condor is informed of his next mission whilst fishing upon his Land Rover in the middle of an inactive volcanic lake!

young hippie girl returns

Arriving in the crowded streets of Barcelona, Condor befriends a young hippie merchant (Shoko Ikeda), who sells whistles and African artefacts. When asked if he will look after her goods for a minute Condor kindly obliges. In her absence Condor sells one of the items to a young German girl (Eva Cobo De Garcia), who unbeknown to her is being watched by a pair of idiotic Arabs who pop in and out throughout the movie. Once the girl leaves, the Arabs get themselves into a petty squabble with Condor over the mysterious item he had sold her. As the Arabs leave the young hippie girl returns before Condor departs to find out the details about his next mission.

Summoned to meet the Duke, Condor is informed of his next mission. The classified information reveals that during the last stages of the Second World War the retreating Nazi forces buried a stockpile of gold looted from all over Europe and stored it in an underground bunker. Condor's mission is to liberate the gold, and he is given a strange ornate key to unlock the gold reserve's vault.

Here Condor is introduced to Ada (played by Carol Do Do Cheng), his partner during the operation. Getting off to a circumspect start with each doubting the other, Condor defies Ada's orders to research the weather conditions of the Sahara, opting instead to look for any living descendants of the missing garrison officers who had stashed the gold.

Arriving at a house that could lead to vital clues, Condor breaks in, though not before an excellent scene where Jackie leaps from one side of the wall to the other in order to clear a gate. This is a great stunt, and one that every true Jackie Chan fan will have attempted at some period in their lives!

escape out of the bathroom

Once inside Jackie begins rummaging through the occupant's possessions before he is ultimately disturbed by their unexpected return. Condor quickly hides in the bathroom, however to his misfortune that's where the occupant needs to go first! Condor realises that the occupant is Eva, the girl he had seen earlier whilst tending to the hippie's stall. What develops next is a great sequence where Jackie does his best to escape out of the bathroom without being detected. He does so finally by sneaking past her when she is washing her face.

Just as Condor is about to leave he hears someone breaking into the apartment and attacking Eva. It turns out it is one of the bumbling Arabs, who chases her around her apartment. Suddenly Condor appears from behind a sheet, beating one of the Arabs into submission. From a small window the Arab's accomplice arrives and forces Condor to back off at gunpoint. Here they disclose the details of their desire to get their hands on the hidden gold. We also discover that Eva's grandfather was the General in charge of the garrison before he and his men went missing.

Threatening to shoot Condor, Condor quickly swipes the towel draped around the girl, leaving her as nature intended. With the Arabs gawking, Condor disarms them before making the pair leave. The girl, who is unimpressed with Condor's actions, then unceremoniously slaps him.

The following day Condor takes the key to a locksmith in order to ascertain its purpose. He is told the key has three parts and that the handle has some part in unlocking the vault's door. He warns Condor that the key could set off a trap unless he can find the right combination.

two thugs accost Condor

By now the Nazi gold seekers are stalking Condor everywhere in order to steal the key. As Condor leaves, two thugs accost Condor at gunpoint. They demand that Condor hand over the key, but Condor kicks one member in the face before escaping.

Riding through the streets of Barcelona on a dirt bike, a truly daredevil and electrifying chase ensues. His pursuers give chase in their black and musty vehicles, with Condor evading them at every turn. Dodging numerous obstacles and twisting and turning down provincial streets, Condor is finally trapped by an array of cars in front of and behind him. The street is so narrow that Condor's only means of escape is to ride over the now stationary vehicles, shattering their windscreens before resuming his escape.

As they reverse back down the alley, Condor steals a bucket of red paint and throws it over the nearest car. A group of tourists are then caught in this melee as the thugs smash into stalls and tables as they continue to hound Condor like a gang of demented dogs. The chase intensifies and a small child in a pram becomes separated from its mother upon a busy road. Stranded in the middle of the road a lorry transporter looks certain to collide with the pram, which would kill the child. Condor, realising the danger, risks his life to save the endangered child. With inches to spare Condor grabs the pram, whisking the child to safety just before the lorry hits an abandoned car.

The sequence also owes a little to Sergei Eisenstein's brilliant 1925 revolutionary classic The Battleship Potemkin. The "Odessa Steps" sequence that is often cited as the best cinematic moment in film history is clearly recognised by Jackie. His interpretation is obviously a cinematic homage showing his appreciation of one of Europe's greatest ever filmmakers. In Eisenstein's version the pram becomes separated from the mother during a massacre by Russian Tsarist troops during the 1905 Russian Revolution. The pram descends down the steps where it crashes at the bottom simultaneously as the uprising is suppressed.

exuberant acrobatic manoeuvres

This magnificent chase culminates on a dock where Condor and his pursuers crash through stacks of boxes inside a giant warehouse. Jackie also demonstrates some exuberant acrobatic manoeuvres as he dodges the hurtling metal of the thugs' cars as he pings around the screen. Finally as vehicles overturn in an orgy of twisted metal, Condor saddles once more on his dirt bike before driving off a pier,

jumping from his bike and clinging onto a block of netted cargo while his pursuers land in the sea where they yell insults at Condor.

Next the film moves to the Sahara where it revs into gear. With Eva joining the group to Ada's disgust, the team arrives at an Arabic hotel. Inside they bicker at the dinner table before Eva storms off. They later discover that their rooms have been trashed, with Ada suspecting Eva is a spy. It transpires that a couple of mercenaries are responsible and they sneak into Ada's room while she is having a shower. Spotting the door's forced entrance Condor investigates. Ada in turn spots a flickering shadow and quickly beats the culprit with a bat. However it turns out to be Condor and they are quickly held captive when the mercenaries emerge from the shadows.

After beating Condor and threatening the pair to get them to hand over the key and classified maps, a bungled attempt to escape results in the capture of Eva. It is then left to Condor to sort the mess out when he distracts their attention by making the mercenaries believe the idiotic Arabs who have congregated outside his room are his backup men. The distraction complete, Condor sends a hair clip into the face of one of the gunmen. A comical passage erupts as the mercenaries and Condor and co wrestle for the priceless key. During the manic escapades that follow, Eva goes berserk with a machine gun, destroying the hotel. With the key safely in their possession they flee.

Next the mercenaries arrive at the hotel headed by Adolf, a former Nazi soldier who is intent on finding the gold. They question the hotelkeeper who informs them they have already left. Meanwhile Condor picks up the young hippie girl who Condor had met in Barcelona. They later set up camp before they are attacked by a gang of ruthless bandits. They kidnap Ada and Eva before escaping. There's a great Jackie moment when he pretends to be killed by a scorpion that displays his comical skills.

At the break of dawn Condor and Ikeda go in search of the bandits' village. Tracking it down they discover the women are going to be auctioned off. However the currency here is not money but camels! After nicking an Arab's clothes Jackie wins back the women whilst getting involved in a small fight where he demonstrates some of his superb moves. Anarchy breaks loose as Ikeda brings down half the village with their Land Rover before escaping. Moments later though they crash, leaving them stranded.

masked gunmen

The storyline turns rather cold when the mercenaries appear at Condor's camp, executing the remaining members. The masked gunmen, showing no remorse, shoot various members of Condor's party (who had joined Condor in his adventures) in the head.

Wandering in the Sahara, those idiotic Arabs catch them and force them to lead them to the hideout. Soon they become lost, and while consulting their map Condor quickly kicks one of the Arabs down a sand dune. The other Arab joins his friend soon after. Condor returns to their camp where they discover the grim bodies of their comrades. Condor buries them, then a change of luck falls upon our heroes. Ikeda recognises the place in Eva's black and white photo of the Nazi garrison, thus leading them to the base.

The base lies inside the ruins of an Arabian encampment. Ikeda leaves to pursue her own journey while the rest of the gang enter the ruins. After being attacked by local tribesmen, Ada unwittingly stumbles upon the Nazi bunker. Inside they discover the remains of the dead soldiers. Meanwhile, Ikeda is kidnapped by the mercenaries and leads them to the base.

Eva discovers that her grandfather was murdered and in his diary it reveals he was forced to give his men poisoned pills in order to conceal the secret of the buried gold. Condor counts the bodies and realises one is missing. Suddenly Adolf arrives and confirms he is the eighteenth soldier and that he murdered Eva's grandfather. Adolf takes them hostage but they immediately escape when Condor slings a dead corpse at his captors.

beautifully choreographed duels

What begins next is a fight of epic and absurd proportions. After some exquisite set pieces using pipes and crates, Jackie's eye towards constructing and crafting beautifully choreographed duels is at its most evident here. In a metallic grid jungle

Jackie's playground generates another feast of explosive martial arts. A bruising and gruelling battle on a gas cylinder ends in a fight on a three part metal structure that resembles a seesaw. As Condor unleashes several deft kicks and punches upon his enemies, he is finally recaptured and led to the bullion's storage room.

With the key now in the hands of the mercenaries they attempt to unlock the door. Condor reveals the combination, however it proves to be incorrect as four machine guns appear from the wall above, gunning down two of Adolf's men. Accused of double crossing them Condor and co are forced to unlock the door. Condor realises that Eva's grandfather's pen number holds the key to unlocking the vault. As the tension mounts Condor holds his nerve and successfully opens the vault.

Inside the mercenaries revel in the amount of gold in their possession. After disarming one mercenary Condor threatens to execute Adolf. His plan backfires though when the rest of the mercenaries form a rebellion against Adolf. Condor is forced to go with the rebel leader. Adolf then traps the rebels by closing the vault's doors.

The final duel then takes place in a giant wind tunnel that is governed by a huge turbine fan. As Condor wrestles against his foes they are blown around like litter. Ada, Eva, Ikeda and Adolf (who's on our side now) control the suction panels, and at one stage they miss the giant fan by inches. However they also activate the self-destruct button! After disposing of the rebels (during a great comical duel in the wind tunnel), Adolf redeems himself by sacrificing his life for the sake of Condor and the girls.

they all eventually become lost!

Trying to escape with some of the gold stash, they are blown to safety through an air shaft moments before the base and gold are blown sky high. With nothing to show for their adventures they stumble across the Arabs they had left in the Sahara. Searching for water they all eventually become lost!

The end duel boasts such innovative thrills that you question what lengths Jackie will go to in order to woo his fans. The end result sent world distributors scampering to get their hands on Operation Condor, and rightly so. Let's hope a third instalment of Operation Condor is not too far way, unlike our poor hero at the end of the film!

Factoids:

The film was co-directed by two longtime Jackie Chan collaborators Chan Chi-wah and Frankie Chan. But it was Jackie who took overall control of the film.

During filming in Morocco, phoney currency used during filming started being used on the streets, resulting in a hefty fine for JC and co, and a spell in prison for the film's production manager.

The western contingent of bad guys included Dan Mintz and Jonathan Isadore (perhaps best known for his role as Mr. Jackson in Jet Li's Once Upon A Time In China, and who would later work with Jackie again on Mr. Nice Guy) as the two bungling Arabs, the mercenaries were played by American martial artists Steve Tartalia, Vincent Lynn, Kenn Goodman and Canadian Wushu maestro Bruce Fontaine (who now trains Chan's Rumble in the Bronx co-star Francoise Yip, in movie fighting and stunts).

Operation Condor was officially released in America before Armour of God, resulting in a switch of titles for its eventual release.

Condor was Jackie's last official sole directorial debut to date. Although large parts of Jackie's subsequent films have been, at least, co-directed by Jackie himself.

Armour of God 3 has been a long talked about project. Frankie Chan spent several months working on the film only for it to be put on hiatus. Advance word on The Accidental Spy is that it looks like a cross between Operation Condor and Who Am I?

JC with Eva Coba De Garcia

DRAGONS FOREVER

EXPLORED!

By Matthew Edwards

Harking back to the format that made "Project A" and "Wheels on Meals" such phenomenal successes, Jackie recruited the talents of the deadly duo Sammo Hung and Yuen Biao, for what was hoped would be another box office bonanza. Reunited for commercial rather than creative reasons, and scheduled for release in the lucrative Chinese New Year, "Dragons Forever" proved to be the last time that the famous trio has worked together to date. However by the end of filming their creative differences had caused their patience with one another to wear thin. Yuen Biao bemoaned afterwards that he felt his role was limited and that the film was merely a showcase for the talents of Jackie and Sammo.

Despite making quiet inroads at the Hong Kong box office, the film however bombed in Japan in much the same way as Chow Yun Fat's change of image in Ringo Lam's masterpiece "Full Contact" caused his film to flop. This scenario was repeated when Jackie's change of image caused his fans to stay away in droves. No one liked the idea of a clean cut Jackie walking around in a suit and tie carrying a brief case, as this was perceived to not fit in with his tough on screen persona. However, as is the trend for Hong Kong movie flops, the film proved to be far more popular here in the West, where it regularly crops up in fans' best of top tens.

In another twist, the trio all played anti-heroes who ultimately redeem themselves. This seemed like somewhat of a departure from Chan's usual good guy roles as he played a scumbag lawyer defending some of Hong Kong's filthiest criminals. As for Sammo's and Yuen's characters, they weren't much better, with Sammo playing a petty crook and gun dealer and Yuen in a wonderful performance as a neurotic cat burglar under therapy!

It all amounts to an exuberant martial-arts swan song that, despite all its flaws and its tendency of falling into the rhetoric of over pompousness (especially early on), still contains some of Jackie's and Sammo's best-choreographed set pieces. Praise should also go to Sammo who again proves that he is not simply an action director, but also a terrific comedy director, for wedged in between the fast and furious action are moments of genuine humour.

one last great showcase

With great additional support from Yuen Wah and Benny "The Jet" Urquidez (although they stupidly reprise their roles from "Eastern Condors" and "Wheels on Meals " respectively), it all equates to (possibly?) one last great showcase from some of Martial Arts' greatest ever performers.

The movie begins as we are introduced to corrupt industrialist Hua (Yuen Wah) who has set up a meeting with a rival crime boss. His rival suspects Hua of foul play as his cargo was stolen and he wants reimbursement. Unable to resolve the situation, Hua bumps his rival off as his henchmen shoot him twice in the chest.

Jackie plays lawyer Johnny Lung, who at the start of the movie is having lunch with a rape victim. Acting on behalf of his client, he offers the woman money to drop the charge. Refusing the offer, she is suddenly attacked by the rapist's henchmen, whereupon Jackie steps in to rescue her. Suddenly a brawl erupts with Jackie sending various henchmen over tables in a grueling and dazzling set piece. At one point he is locked in a bear hug before he superbly elbows the thug in the face and thus is sent sprawling onto the ground.

When one of the henchmen threatens to kidnap the young girl by bundling her into his vehicle, Jackie is seen jumping from a balcony in slow motion onto a stationary vehicle, whereupon he frees the girl, who in turn pushes the thug into a river! However, believing Mr. Lung was in on the set up she proceeds to slap him across the face, whereupon Jackie slaps her back!

In court, Jackie incredibly manages to get the yuppie rapist off the hook, whereupon beset by guilt he slams a fist into the rapist's gut immediately after the case has been closed (this still does little to redeem him). We also discover that Jackie's character is a sleazy womanizer, who seems to try it on with every woman he meets.

The fact that Jackie plays an excessive philanderer may have also contributed to the film's overriding failure in Asia. For his hordes of female followers (especially in Japan) this may not have fitted into the perception of how they viewed their idol. Seeing him as this lowlife character who lacked any respect for women was not a notion they appreciated, nor were willing to accept.

Meanwhile fish hatchery owner Miss Yeh (Deanie Yip), who accuses Hua of polluting her lake and killing her fish, threatens to take out a court injunction against the cigar puffing Hua. Hua offers to buy the lake from Miss Yeh, however she refuses outright, claiming she would not sell to a scumbag like him. Suddenly out of the blue, and to Mr. Hua's surprise, she offers to buy his factory, whereupon he rudely declines. Unable to come to a compromise, Mr. Hua declares "I'll meet you in court", before professing he will employ a corrupt lawyer to defend him. Enter Jackie!

Impressed the thugs

In the next scene we are introduced to Fei (played by the marvelous Sammo Hung) who has set up a deal with a pair of shady crooks. Within the confines of a decrepid old warehouse Sammo gets on with his arms deal. Pulling various semi automatic weapons from his clapped out green holdall, he even goes as far as testing out the weapons, shooting off hundreds of rounds of ammunition into the roof's interiors. Impressed but unable to pay Fei cash, the thugs offer to pay him on credit. Fei cheekily offers them a couple of rusty butcher's knives instead. Insulted and sensing an opportunity to kill Sammo they attack him, however they are both sent crashing into the empty crates as Fei unleashes several lightening kicks, with one of the thugs receiving a brutal blow to his forehead. As they both writhe pathetically upon the floor, Fei boasts that no-one can out smart him.

Leaving the isolated warehouse, Fei gets a call on his mobile from Jackie who requests assistance from Fei in his forthcoming case against Miss Yeh. The pair meet upon a small boat outside Miss Yeh's fish hatchery. At the same time, with the help of her colleagues, Miss Yeh sprays a group of Hua's business partners who have come to buy the property from her, with a large hose, and they crash into the river. With Fei agreeing to take up the assignment, the pair leaves.

Next up we meet Tung Te-Piao (Yuen Biao), who comes peddling in on a small bicycle with a large ladder attached (I told you he was neurotic). Stopping outside his apartment, which sports a giant neon Kodak advertising board, Tung bizarrely enters his apartment using his ladder like chopsticks. Wandering in he spots the shadow of Johnny, and suspecting him of being an intruder, he decides to attack him.

What ensues is a very amusing duel as Tung lays into Johnny, as he suspects he is being burgled. Despite the fact that Johnny yells his name out about twenty times, because of the darkness Tung is not convinced, instead opting to pound Johnny's body with several furious punches. It is only when Johnny opens up a fridge that Tung, realising who it is, finally begins to calm himself down.

After spouting off a load of jargon

Tung's room is revealed to be tech heaven with its two-foot light switch and transparent cylinder tubes in which fish swim up and down. After spouting off a load of jargon about fish being Communists, Johnny finally gets a word in edge ways and he informs Tung of a job he needs doing. It transpires that Tung is needed to bug Miss Yeh's home, which he gleefully agrees to.

Having recruited both Fei and Tung they set out to spy on Miss Yeh and her cousin Wen Mei-Ling, played by Pauline Yeung. The matter gets further complicated when Johnny starts to put the moves on Miss Yeh's cousin, who he keeps asking out constantly. However, Johnny's two bumbling

Jackie in angry mode - the finale of 'Dragons Forever'

sidekicks can't be in the same room together without getting into a fight.

This is exemplified in the next scene, after we have discovered Fei has moved in next door, when Tung arrives to bug the room for Lung. Fei who is also bugging Miss Yeh's room believes that Tung is a burglar, and thus proceeds to attack him. The ensuing kerfuffle brings their presence to the attention of Miss Yeh and Mei-Ling, who rally together and smash a pot over Tung's head! Thanking Fei, they promptly call the police.

Arrested and released on bail, Tung is, unsurprisingly, not too pleased with Lung. However, things go from bad to worse when Lung, who has managed to invite Mei-Ling over for a dinner invitation, has both Tung and Fei turning up unexpectedly (Yuen has only turned up to ask Lung why he is such a neurotic, much to Lung's amazement). Believing he has got rid of Tung, Fei suddenly arrives. This causes problems as Fei is meant to be Mei-Ling's new neighbour. Making sure his cover isn't blown Lung attempts to hide Sammo in a cramped cupboard! Unable to breath inside, Fei falls out, only to see Tung. Needless to say they begin fighting again much to Lung's disgust.

as they wrestle maniacally on the sofa

Fei believes Tung is burgling Lung's home, thus they continue their feud with each other, as they wrestle maniacally on the sofa or behind doors. It's always good to see Yuen and Sammo squaring up to one another, especially when they are ruthlessly throwing each other over their shoulders onto pinewood tables, making it a shame they don't do it more often.

Unable to cope with his pals' excessive bungling, Lung brings his date to a close. However, Mei-Ling returns to get her cardigan midway through a three-way fight involving Lung, Tung and Fei! With a black eye and bleeding nose, Lung quickly palms Mei-Ling off, more intent on sorting out his conflicting buddies. In this comic interlude they all start pounding the stuffing out of each other, that again highlights Jackie's and Sammo's ability to inject humour into their choreography.

As they all sit sulking battered and bruised in a cocktail bar, Lung discusses the deal and their twenty percent cut. Lung comments that he will seduce Miss Mei-Ling in order to get Miss Yeh to drop the charges against Hua. As an uneasy tension mounts between Fei and Tung, who have continued their bickering, Hua enters the bar with his men.

Lung introduces Hua to Fei and Tung and informs Hua that they are helping him collect evidence against Miss Yeh. Hua comments that he is glad that Lung is defending him, otherwise he would be dead. However, Yuen starts an argument with Hua's henchmen and then goes somewhat berserk. Unsurprisingly a fight erupts inside the club. As tables fly, Jackie and co lay into Hua's henchmen, as the discotheque becomes less trendy by the second. After everything calms down, Lung apologises to Hua.

What transpires is a failed assassination attempt on an elaborate yacht.

A price is suddenly put on Lung's head, as they want him out of the picture. What transpires is a failed assassination attempt on an elaborate yacht. Poor old Lung is having little luck dating Mei-Ling as he is subsequently attacked. Climbing aboard the ship the thugs attack Lung wielding machetes. Dodging countless swipes, Lung is chased religiously up and down the yacht's decks, immobilising various members by smacking wicker chairs around their heads or throwing them from balconies. Lung spectacularly disposes of one of the members when he sends him flying out of a window into the sea below. Mei-Ling returns oblivious to the previous madness before departing.

romance begins to blossom

At this point in the film the romance begins to blossom as Lung falls for Miss Mei-Ling and Sammo for Miss Yeh (he invites her to dinner by using a megaphone in Hong Kong's busy streets). Lung also admits that he is defending Hua, before professing his love for Mei-Ling. Well isn't this all swell!

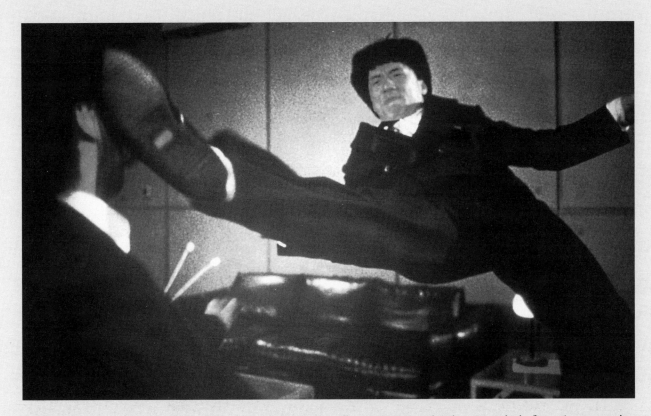

After Tung is told by bank robbers to kill all the witnesses who got him arrested (he thought it was the doctor!), he sneaks into Lung's home to kill Mei-Ling. Dressed as a cat burglar, Lung spots him and a mini tussle begins. Pulling off his mask, Lung discovers it's Tung, whereupon, just as Miss Yeh and Sammo arrive, he lets slip about the threesome bugging their home and their attempt to make Miss Yeh sell her business. Needless to say our lovebirds are unceremoniously dumped.

Somewhat aggrieved with Tung, Sammo belts Tung around the face sending him spiraling to the ground. Suddenly within the car park, all three begin fighting one another. Amidst scenes of bruising martial arts and slapstick comedy, they all launch dynamic scissor kicks and punches into each other's midriffs. As the soft tissue around their faces and groins becomes redder and bloodier, Miss Yeh calls the police.

This scene boasts some superbly choreographed fight sequences as Jackie, Sammo and Yuen all beat the hell out of each other. There seems to be no rhythm or structure to the brawl, but that's the brilliant trick as it is beautifully staged. They seem intent on bashing each other. Each trying to be the first one to get back up on their feet. At one point Sammo and Jackie work in tandem to knock Yuen to the floor, before proceeding to attack each other.

Thankfully our immature imbeciles are merely cautioned and freed by the police. Fei and Tung finally become friends, and with his assistance Fei goes to check out Hua's factory. This is not before Fei jumps out in front of Miss Yeh's vehicle, and is subsequently struck with a savage blow to the forehead with a spanner. As the crimson blood runs down his cheek they both make up.

superb slow-motion

Fei and Tung break into Hua's factory and discover it's a big heroin refinery. Whilst taking photographic evidence, Fei is spotted and surrounded by Hua's men. Quizzed in respect of his presence there, Fei tries to leave discreetly, before he ultimately ends up taking on the entire plant. With the sheer ease by which he disposes of most of the henchmen (one member is sent backwards into a glass window in superb slow-motion by a delightful Sammo kick), it would seem escape was a formality.

To his misfortune though in steps Benny "The Jet" Urquidez. Wearing eyeliner and make up, Benny looks like death with his sunken beady eyes.

Clicking his neck he revs into action. After a mini fistfight he sends a cruising kick into Fei's chest, sending him to the floor where he is strung up and given an overdose.

Meanwhile in court, the case is suspended when Mei-Ling admits to loving Lung. With the case withdrawn, Tung gathers Lung and co and sets about rescuing Fei, who has been heavily drugged.

Mei-Ling even goes bananas with a nunchaku

Bursting into the factory, they confront Hua. As they are about to leave, Fei sends a chair crashing through a window in order to warn Lung that it is a narcotics dump. What ensues is a frenzied end fight sequence that is peppered with numerous slow motion kicks that leave you in a state of awe. Mei-Ling even goes bananas with a nunchaku.

Bodies are strewn lifeless as they fall from the steel staircases and balconies onto the brightly coloured gas cylinders below. A battered Lung at one stage sends one henchman backward into a white glass coffee table, shattering it immediately. Meanwhile Benny beats Yuen senseless when he sends a stunning spinning scissor kick right into Yuen's upper torso. The fact that it is shown in slow motion makes it even more spectacular. Badly wounded, Yuen lies motionless.

Facing a two-prong attack from Hua and Benny, Jackie strips to his more familiar attire. A mini-duel erupts, where both receive brutal blows (at one stage Jackie produces a superb two-footed kick that sends Benny into an array of empty boxes).

After Hua beats up Mei-Ling, he is finally disposed off when Fei stabs a syringe into Hua's neck. Convulsing manically, Hua is thrown over Fei's shoulder into a giant vat of toxic waste.

Finally Jackie and Benny square off against each other. As the gruelling fight almost overcomes the pair of them, Jackie pulls out enough strength to send Benny flinging backwards into a glass cabinet where he is electrocuted. As they pull out of the factory injured and dazed, and women in tow, the police arrive on the scene.

The last fifteen minutes prove to be a revelation, and extremely violent. The scene boasts great feats of showmanship from all three of our Peking buddies. The trio by the end of the movie are exonerated from their earlier crafty deeds. The real high point still remains, although the duel is slightly rehashed from "Wheels on Meals", the duel between "The Jet" and Jackie. Let's hope a reunion is not too far around the corner, from all those concerned.

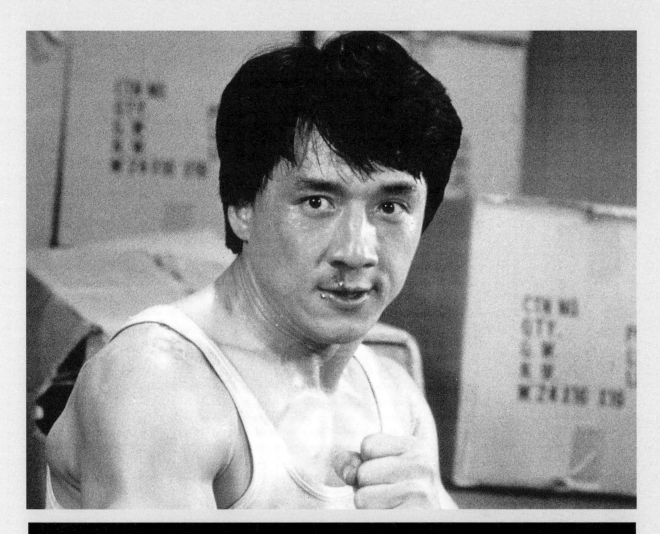

Factoids:

The Japanese title for Dragons Forever is Cyclone Z, following on from Wheels on Meals which was known as Spartan-X, which later became the name of Renee Witterstaetter's comic book adventures of Jackie Chan.

The refinery setting for the finale of Dragons Forever would later turn up as the location for the original ending of Golden Harvest's Cynthia Rothrock actioner Blonde Fury/Lady Reporter. Originally directed by actor turned choreographer Mang Hoi, the film's original finale pitted Mang Hoi and Chin Siu-ho against kickboxer Billy Chow, while la Rothrock battled a real Thai Boxing champion. The film was taken over by Dragons director Corey Yuen who shot additional action for a whole new finale.

Longtime Jackie Chan stunt-teamer Man Ching can be seen in Dragons sporting a lovely bouffant haircut.

Crystal Kwok would later go on to interview Jackie Chan for sections of Jackie Chan: My Story.

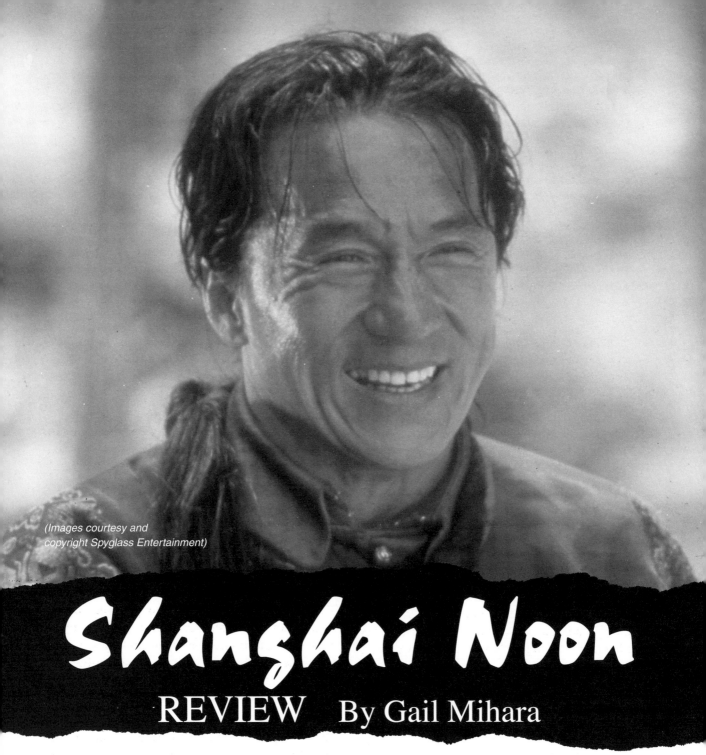

(Images courtesy and copyright Spyglass Entertainment)

Shanghai Noon
REVIEW   By Gail Mihara

For years, Jackie Chan talked about making his dream film - a sprawling Western follow-ing the exploits of a man from China who travels to the wilds of 1800s America. Along the way he loses his memory and gains not only a Native American wife, but also a Chinese wife and more than his share of trouble. Every year Jackie would produce new and innovative work - spy thrillers, racing flicks, romances… but no Westerns. The film, tentatively titled "Lion Goes West", seemed destined to forever remain on his "to do" list, a great film that could have been, but wasn't. Until now, that is…

With the success of "Rush Hour" firmly under his belt, Jackie finally has some clout, and the trust of his Hollywood producers to bring his heretofore dream movie to reality in "Shanghai Noon". An irreverently reverent (if that's possible!) take on the classic Western (as well as a few other genres), "Shanghai Noon" is fun summer entertainment in its purest form.

Jackie plays Chon Wang (sounds like "John Wayne" - geddit?), loyal member of the Chinese Imperial Guard. When Princess Pei Pei (Lucy Liu) is spirited away from the Forbidden City during his watch, he manages to talk his way onto the official entourage delivering the ransom to her captors.

On a steam train bound for the ransom drop in Carson City, Nevada, Chon encounters wannabe superstar bandit Roy O'Bannon (Owen Wilson). Less concerned with robbing trains than with looking great while doing it, Roy is an easygoing gloryhound with a penchant for new age philosophy and brothel babes.

The pair get off to a rocky start when Roy's temporary gang robs the train and tries to kill Jackie. But after this early misunderstanding, Jackie (eager to bring the Princess home) and Roy (just as eager to get his hands on the gold ransom) join forces, and the fun begins.

Liberated by "Rush Hour" from the invisible shackles of Hollywood's preconceived notions, Jackie approaches the role of Chon with his patented combination of intricate rough and tumble action and pure comedy. "Shanghai Noon" is his baby, and it shows.

Whereas in "Rush Hour" Jackie seemed more like an employee on his first day at the job - impeccably groomed, on his best behaviour, eager to show what he can do, but ultimately reserved because of the newness of the situation - in "Shanghai Noon" he finally cuts loose. Whether he is frolicking in a bubble bath, enjoying a kiss of gratitude from a brothel employee or having a deep philosophical conversation with his horse, this Jackie is freer and more joyous than his previous forays on the American screen.

When the casting for "Shanghai Noon" was announced, the immediate response from many fans was, "Owen who?" Those familiar with Owen Wilson's eye-catching work in "Bottle Rocket" and "Armageddon" were more optimistic. In Wilson, the filmmakers wisely chose to avoid the temptation to copy the Chan/Tucker combination. In fact, the actor/writer could be considered the 'anti-Tucker' by comparison.

Tall and lanky, with a laconic way and a generous spirit, Wilson's anachronistically mellow Roy O'Bannon is the perfect companion for Jackie's Chon Wang. Not above taking time out of a robbery to show off his six-shooter to a pretty girl, he lives for the notoriety of being a bad boy, though he is not nearly as bad as he thinks he is. "Do you know what this says?" he asks Chon when they spot a wanted poster with O'Bannon's picture on it. "It says, 'Drives girls crazy!'"

Jokes aside, Roy's respect for Chon is extremely reassuring. Instead of making jokes at the Imperial Guard's expense and talking circles around him for comedy's sake, the bank robber wannabe is fascinated. This open-mindedness permeates the whole film, leaving a warm glow. While the movie may be cheeky in its political incorrectness, this is one area where there is no room for humour. The one time O'Bannon does make a racial slip, it threatens the whole relationship. That Wilson's character can insult Jackie without becoming unlikeable is a credit to the actor's skill.

The rest of the cast is strong, though as decreed by buddy movie law, all must take a backseat to the buddies in question. Roger Yuan does a good job as the Imperial Guard traitor who masterminds the princess's capture, but he doesn't log quite enough screen time to give his eventual defeat much emotional heft.

There is even less time given to the women, as their main function is to act as devices to keep the plot moving. Brandon Merrill as Chon Wang's stoic Native American bride personifies this concept, as she is rarely seen in the film unless the pair needs rescuing. Otherwise she is presumably somewhere in the woods, out of camera range, finding new clothes to change into after each scene.

Lucy Liu is a formidable presence as Princess Pei Pei, and she does the most she can with the material, but she is ultimately merely the prize everyone is fighting over. Opportunities arise near the end for her to show off her kickboxing skills and prove her mettle, but she spends much of the film just being beautifully defiant. Fortunately, her pluckiness promises good things should her character be brought back for the sequel.

Fans of Jackie's kung fu fighting will be pleased to know that "Shanghai Noon" is blessed with six fight sequences. Though not nearly as long nor as complex as his homegrown efforts, they are still the best in the biz. The JC action team under the guidance of longtime Chan friend and Hong Kong legend Yuen Biao do their usual splendid kick-ass job keeping the pace fast and furious, and very entertaining.

Train Rumble: A literal running battle between Chon and Roy's boys that barrels its way along the insides and topsides of several train cars. Not "Drunken Master 2", but the next best thing.

Forest Fight: A fine piece that starts in a river and ends up in the woods, as Chon Wang dukes it out with a group of fierce Crow warriors. In this sequence he literally creates weapons from the environment as he takes down several opponents with the spruces surrounding him. A fine blend of razor-sharp action and lighting-fast comedy.

Saloon Brawl: What everyone has been waiting for. After all, a Western isn't a Western without a knock-down, drag-out saloon fight, and "Shanghai Noon" doesn't disappoint. In this sequence Jackie utilises a stuffed grizzly bear, a set of antlers and various chairs, stools and tables to get the job done.

Chon and Roy Vs. the Posse: Jackie makes use of a rope and a horseshoe to take down three armed opponents. Just another day at the office. Classic Hong Kong stuff, though the rope blends into the background a bit, making the movements difficult to follow.

Miners' Camp: The first fisticuffs confrontation between Jackie and the evil villain, but actually intended as an appetiser before the big battle.

Mission Wrap-Up: The grand finale as Roy and Chon must confront their respective enemies. Chon's running fight involves some long-awaited and very impressive sword and spear work (which makes Roy's stationary gun battle look rather pedestrian by comparison). But the overall result is very Hollywood and very satisfying.

"Shanghai Noon" has even more going for it than just spectacular fisticuffs. In addition to sparkling character interaction and snappy dialogue, it is blessed with a moral conscience, managing to touch upon a very real issue - that of self-determination.

The East saddles up to go West:
JC's dream project becomes a reality

The Princess flees the Imperial City to avoid an arranged marriage. Once in America she chooses to stay and help the railroad slaves find freedom. Chon Wang is torn between his duty and what he knows is right. In fact, the only time he falters is when he is following the iron-clad rules of the Imperial Guard. In the Forbidden City he is a slave. In America he is free. In the end he must choose which edict to follow, that of China or his own. This is just one of the many fine touches in a movie that's all the more impressive as it's from a director making his feature film début, Tom Dey.

Technically, the film is a visual treat, brave enough to take the organic approach in an age when quick cutting visuals are the norm rather than the exception. Cinematographer Dan Mindel takes his time to imbue the natural spectacles - towering mountain tops, rushing rivers, cool forests - with a substance and majesty that lends depth and credence to the story.

Movie buffs will find much to enjoy here, as the film is a virtual cornucopia of hat tips to classic movies, from the church belltower scene in "Vertigo" to the Mexican standoff in "Butch Cassidy and the Sundance Kid" to the Chevy Chase "Be the ball" monologue in "Caddyshack". There's even a take from "Drunken Master 2", not to mention the joke contained within the film's title. "Shanghai Noon" could be considered a kinder and gentler grandson of the king of Western comedies, "Blazing Saddles". What other movie would feature a horse that gets plastered on whiskey? Even "Shanghai Noon"'s score is double-take close to the "Saddles" theme.

Parents need not worry that the Americanisation of Jackie will make him less family friendly. "Shanghai Noon" is suitable for kids of all ages, though there is a token smattering of the "s" word by the bad guys. Otherwise there is precious little blood, guts, or nekkid flesh.

With not one but two sequels reportedly already in the planning stages, the filmmakers have their work cut out for them. But as long as they stay true to Jackie's vision of bringing the East to the West, no doubt we will all be able to look forward to the rip roarin' adventures of Chon Wang and Roy O'Bannon for many years to come.

What the critics say...

"[Jackie Chan] is a human special effect. And as always, he gives a full measure of devotion to his blindingly choreographed action sequences. Increasingly, though, we go to Jackie Chan movies not for the star's good moves but for his good nature."
Richard Shickel, Time magazine

"A sparkling showcase for Jackie Chan's genius for physical comedy and a breakout role for Owen Wilson."
Jonathan Foreman, New York Post

"As usual, Chan is nothing less than poetry in motion, evidencing graceful exuberance in his physical comedy and cunning inventiveness in his fight scenes."
Joe Leydon, Variety

"Jackie Chan... is an entertainer whose appeal transcends differences of culture, age and taste... "Shanghai Noon" is, in classic Western tradition, a celebration of male bonding, unabashedly juvenile, boyishly risqué and disarmingly sweet."
A. O. Scott, New York Times

"Jackie Chan and Owen Wilson... are the funniest Western heroes to hit town since "Blazing Saddles"; actually they're funnier, because the movie's comic spirit is so much sweeter."
Wall Street Journal

RUSH HOUR 2
Review

By Gail Mihara

(Movie images courtesy of New Line Cinema)

When "Rush Hour" came out in 1998, it caused a sensation, shocking Hollywood by raking in an amazing $33 million during its opening weekend alone. Considering the considerable box-office take, this franchise bonanza in the making was a natural for a sequel, which everyone assumed would arrive in short order.

Three years later, mismatched cops Lee and Carter have finally decided to make a return appearance in "Rush Hour 2", which raked in a stupefying $66.8 million in its opening weekend. A few weeks later, that total had increased to $200 million. (Can anyone say, "Rush Hour 3"?) Without embarking on the topic of sequels to sequels, suffice to say this sequel starts where the original left off, with Hong Kong inspector Lee (Jackie Chan) and LAPD detective Carter (Chris Tucker) enjoying a well-earned vacation in Lee's home town. Unfortunately, to Lee this means dragging the American along on various investigations when he would rather be picking up local mushu (Carter-ese for "booty").

But there is no time for mushu or indeed boo-tay when Lee is ordered to track down a beautiful female bomber, who has blown up the US consulate. Naturally, the US secret service provides patronising "this is our case so keep out of the way" interference, causing the local Hong Kong cops to do a little digging on their own.

Discovering that a Triad bigwig named Ricky Tan (John Lone) might have something to do with the bombing, Lee goes after the mobster with a cranky, complaining Carter in tow. Thus begins a series of misadventures and misunderstandings, with Lee trying desperately to discover what link Tan has with the explosion, and Carter trying desperately to avoid police work.

Much to the cops' dismay, however, while they're going after Tan, Tan comes after them, in the form of the mobster's deadly psycho henchchick Hu Li (Zhang Ziyi), whose main joy in life seems to be beating, shooting, stabbing, blowing stuff up and generally causing great inconvenience to others.

The McGuffin all this mayhem is for is a set of plates that can be used to create surprisingly realistic but fake US currency. Tan and Co. are smuggling said phoney cash to the States, for laundering at a Chinese-themed Vegas casino run by a rich mogul with the pun-tastic name of "Reign" (played by American comedian Alan King). Also on hand is Reign's plaything Isabella Molina (Roselyn Sanchez), who is actually an undercover secret service agent with a penchant for enticing lingerie.

One feels a bit sorry for Lee and Carter this time around as they are kidnapped, beaten up, blown up, skewered, and joyfully abused before the film's big bang climax (which has a few extra stunts tossed in for crunch, like croutons).

Less focused on plot than the original, "Rush Hour 2" is a nervy stream-of-consciousness roller-coaster of thrills, chills and laughs. Taking advantage of a beefed up budget, the sequel takes the original's most successful aspects and does them bigger and better - and louder.

Loudest of all is Chris Tucker. His Carter is still just as wild, wired, and whupass as ever, except this time around he finds himself out of his element in the wilds of Hong Kong. The new environment doesn't faze him, however. In fact, it makes him even more determined to wrangle control over his situation, be it on the karaoke stage doing a hilarious Michael Jackson impersonation, or in the street markets of Hong Kong, where he battles a poultry vendor over the fate of a squawking chicken. But the consummate Tucker-ian moment comes on his home turf of America, where he distracts the bad guys with a deliriously goofy verbal tirade about racially discriminatory casino chip distribution that stops the show.

Jackie is on fine form as usual, bringing back all of Lee's best qualities: decency, compassion, guts and bravery (while thankfully abandoning his original slicked hair). Decked out in Lee's trademark Regis Philbin suits, Jackie is not only given the opportunity to showcase his considerable physical prowess, but he also displays his dramatic range. As the film's emotional anchor, he gives the movie the heart that would otherwise be lacking. By showing the audience how much he cares for Carter, he lends Tucker's character a depth it wouldn't normally have on its own. Jackie even manages to toss some potent comedy into the mix, such as when Lee is seen listening to P. Diddy's 'I'll Be Missing You' after an extremely hard day in the office.

The chemistry between the two stars - so fundamental to the success of the original film - has actually improved the second time around. Whereas the first "Rush Hour" saw the two strong personalities feeling each other out, by the second film they have fallen into a very friendly, comfortable rhythm. This doesn't mean they don't bicker, however. If anything, they're fighting even more than ever, much to the delight of the audience.

Joining the antics this time is John Lone ("The Last Emperor") as the evil Ricky Tan. A gentleman gangster with a significant connection to Lee's life, Tan is the stereotype-defying one in the tux who throws out a few *bon mots* before waving in his henchmen to beat the crap out of Lee and Carter.

Zhang Ziyi is pure pissed-off evil as Tan's henchgirl Hu Li. Dressed as a stereotypical dragon lady, she is offered little in the way of character development. But who needs character development when you can fight like that? Tough, ruthless, deadly and completely insane, she is happiest when causing wanton destruction. But she looks good doing it, so it's OK.

In keeping with the sequel's "bigger is better" mentality, Elizabeth Peña's presence as the only girl cop in the first film has been replaced by the taller, younger, and more curvaceous delights of Roselyn Sanchez as secret service agent Molina, giving both Lee and Carter an object of long-legged desire to drool over with abandon. The actress injects the character with plenty of attitude as she saves the heroes' lives, and gives them clues while dressed in little black panties!

Plus, there is some hint of a spark between her and Lee that (hopefully) could be addressed in the next film - if Jackie has anything to say about it, that is. Reportedly the action star suggested to the director that something a bit more steamy than an innocent kiss between Lee and Molina might be in order. Unfortunately for Jackie, that suggestion was shot down. Maybe next time...

Some familiar faces pop up in the supporting roles: Lee's chief is played by Kenneth Tsang, who played the villain Chaibat in "Super Cop", and longtime JC Group staffer and bit part player William Tuen has a funny turn as a sneaky taxi driver who fleeces Carter. One face that's missing, however, is Chris Penn, earlier announced to be making a return appearance as Clive, the explosives merchant with a heart. He is nowhere to be seen.

JC and Chis Tucker in a tight spot in 'Rush Hour 2'

Fortunately Jackie's stunt boys are back, helping the boss to pull off a series of brief fighting sequences that top the ones in the original film and really help bring this movie to life:

Bamboo Scaffold Fight: Jackie gives American audiences a tantalising taste of this Hong Kong movie staple (though the night scene lighting and too-close camera work make the choreography hard to fully appreciate). Lee chases Hu Li and numerous familiar faces from the stunt squad up a bamboo scaffold, doing battle with the bad guys as the astonished tenants try to have dinner.

Massage Parlour Fight: A new and improved version of Jackie's "Protector" Hong Kong massage parlour fight. Tucker joins in the action here, extending and elaborating on the fancy fisticuffs seen in "Rush Hour". Jackie's pyrotechnic acrobatics highlight this battle.

Red Dragon Yacht Fight: A quickie to kill a few minutes, in which Jackie dukes it out with some evil henchmen on the edge of a moving boat. Ever the gentleman even when faced with evil, Jackie does his best to help the bad guys when they're in danger of toppling into the water.

Chinese Soul Kitchen Scuffle: A mini-scuffle between Jackie and one of Carter's many backroom card game-running informants, played by Don Cheadle in a much-publicised but uncredited cameo appearance. A major Chan fan, Cheadle reportedly refused to take the role unless he could have a fight scene with the action hero, which he pulls off with much flair. Along with the kung fu training he took up for the film, he also manages to deliver some very comprehensible Cantonese. (One hopes Don might show up in "Rush Hour 3".)

Cash Room Fight: Featured in many commercials and promotional clips for the film, this battle pits Jackie against the security guards of a Las Vegas casino. A fiery (yet all-too-brief) acrobatic display involving cabinet doors, chips and cold hard cash, the gorgeous highlight is a smooth exit by Chan through the slot in a banker's window.

Girl Fight: Of course it had to happen. Every teenage boy's fantasy comes true when Sanchez and Zhang cross stilettos and tussle a bit.

Casino Fight: Not exactly a fight, but much action

JC on fighting form in a massage parlour

and confusion ensues when the casino patrons make a panicked, mass exodus while Lee tries to find the detonator for a bomb that's taped into his mouth. (You'll have to see the movie!)

Carter vs Girl: Astonishingly, there is no fight between Jackie and Zhang, leaving us with Tucker and some what-might-have-beens. Still, this is a top-notch comic duel, with Carter winning by default.

Final Mini-Fight: As if to make up for the lack of a Zhang/Chan match-up, Jackie is given a little drama/tussle with main villain John Lone. The emphasis is more on drama and emotions this time around, however, but Chan's performance is just as strong.

"Rush Hour 3" is already in the works, with talk of it taking place in Egypt, or some other location where not just one but both detectives will be fish out of water. Until that far away day, however, Chan fans must content themselves with "Rush Hour 2", which has turned out to be one of the major blockbusters of the summer. (And how can it not be with Screen Power staff member Renee Witterstaeter on the crew as a production assistant?)

JACKIE IN LONDON

Jackie Chan hit town in July 2001 to promote "Rush Hour 2", prior to the start of filming on "Highbinders" in Ireland. Screen Power Editor Richard Cooper caught up with his boss, the one and only Jackie Chan. He originally wanted to interview Jackie about the film, but Jackie was doing a number of interviews about "Rush Hour 2" on his two-day London junket, and seemed far more interested in the idea of an informal chat that would be more personal, and very much more exclusive to the worldwide readership of everyone's favourite magazine - Screen Power… Read on!

JC takes a keen interest in Screen Power

Tuesday, 10 July 2001. It's an early start on a somewhat (but typical) overcast British summer day! It takes just under two hours to reach London from Bath by car, but we take no chances: our meeting with Jackie is at 3:20pm, but we head off at 10:30am. For this trip (or adventure, it's all the same to me) I am joined by our new recruit Paul Williams.

Paul couldn't believe his luck when I told him that his first assignment for Screen Power was to accompany me up to London to interview Jackie! I don't think he stopped smiling all day... Be sure to check out Paul's own diary of his meeting with The Chanster in Jade Screen (our new sister publication), together with a few different photos! Do we publish the two best magazines in the world or what?

We arrive in London in good time... which is just as well as we end up circling Park Lane, Piccadilly Circus and Hyde Park for over an hour trying to find somewhere to park! In such times a good sense of humour is a must...

Jackie has been in his hotel from the early morning, conducting a series of interviews for various newspapers and magazines. In fact he was doing an interview every ten minutes! I guess that's the price (or punishment) for being a superstar.

Around 3:10pm we walk upstairs to Jackie's suite and I ring the doorbell. We are greeted with a smile and invited in by Linda Russell, the UK-based publicist for the "Rush Hour 2" junket, and told to sit and relax as Jackie is just finishing off another interview.

Shortly afterwards, the man himself walks into the lounge room laughing and smiling. He's decked out in black Chinese garb complete with pulled back cuffs on his sleeves. All five feet eight inches of solid muscle almost crushes the life out of me when we greet each other with a hug.

I introduce Paul to Jackie and they shake hands. As a surprise to Paul, Jackie asks him whether they had met before... A very shocked Paul nods his head! They did meet once, very briefly, at a fans' gathering I organised a couple of years ago at London's Planet Hollywood. "Either Jackie has an amazing memory or he was just being polite and he says that to everyone he meets!" remarks Paul later on. Either way, Paul is a happy man.

Richard Cooper with
the man himself, Jackie Chan

Jackie tells us to follow him into the next room. "It's better in here, and there are more comfy seats!" Jackie tells us as we follow him next door to the suite's meeting room. "I've been here from this morning talking to about thirty reporters about "Rush Hour 2"… So boring… Let's not talk about "Rush Hour 2" in here… People can watch the movie and make up their own minds!" Jackie sits down and starts pouring out some coffee.

I start laughing and tell Jackie that, unfortunately, I have a number of questions about "Rush Hour 2" to ask him. He laughs out loud. "No! We can talk about other things! I will not talk to the reporters about these kind of things, but we will talk about it. That's much better." I have to agree. I sit down with Paul, press record on my tape recorder and place it on the table.

So, here it is, exactly as it took place. Not really an interview, more of a friendly conversation. It's candid, revealing, and totally exclusive to Screen Power:

Screen Power:
Jackie, so here we are in London, You are here for just two days promoting your new Hollywood movie, "Rush Hour 2".
Jackie Chan:
Yes!
SP: *You travel so much these days. Does Hong Kong still feel like home to you, even though you travel all over the world with your work?*
JC: Yes, but… (short pause) I don't like Hong Kong anymore!

SP: Why not?
JC: Because of all the paparazzi. Yeah, they're really horrifying, you know. It's terrible, they just follow me wherever I go. And I don't feel safe anymore!

SP: It's that bad?
JC: Yeah! If we have a meeting in a restaurant then they will make up a story, you know, and the next day in the newspapers and the magazines, it's "Oh Jackie! In a nightclub, with young girls!" I hate it! Because you know I am always, and will always, be against the paparazzi. I say a lot but now all the paparazzi, the magazines, the newspapers - they all fight me back! I get so angry…

SP: But you are the Tourist Ambassador of Hong Kong! I can't understand why they do that. They should support you…
JC: Yes… the audience knows that. But they keep doing these things to me, and I really don't like it… Even if I go back to Australia to visit my Mum - the paparazzi are already there!

SP: Already?
JC: Yes! Waiting for me! When I leave the airport they follow me! "What's my address?"… "Jackie, what's your home number?" They ask me this! That's a terrible thing…

SP: What about your wife and your son? Do they understand about the paparazzi?
JC: Yes, it's why they're hiding! I'm a human being. I have a family, but I am a star too, but still I want to protect my family… What can I do? The press are so powerful. They can use the pen everyday to write about you. You have to either surrender, or you can fight back! But, how much of my energy should I use to fight them back with? No! I would rather waste my energy in a movie instead. So this is why I get away from Hong Kong; then I am happy. I'm so happy now. Now I'm in England. London. With you, talking… Now I can feel safe and relax. I am going to Paris the day after tomorrow, then Dublin, then Toronto… Good! You know, when I go to LA, the paparazzi stay outside my house, my bodyguards walk two steps and they just run away…

SP: **Does everyone know where you live in LA?**

JC: Yes! I don't like it…

SP: **Well it's certainly true then that when you become a superstar you cannot lead a normal life.**

JC: You know, I think even America, I don't know about England - the paparazzi, they never…

SP: **Princess Diana… she was a victim of the English paparazzi…**

JC: Yes, very sad. You don't ever say to people where you are staying… which floor… what your car number is… where your son goes to school. That means you tell bad people everything… It can lead to kidnap! We do have kidnapping going on right now in Hong Kong! It's so bad…

SP: **You really are travelling so much these days, in fact you spend half the month on a plane, and you live in hotel rooms like this don't you?**

JC: (Sips a cup of coffee) Yeah. But the base is still in Hong Kong. My offices… But, you know me (laughing), I always travel, travel, travel, travel. Almost non-stop!

SP: **I hate planes and flying, and I only fly every couple of months but for you it's crazy!**

JC: (Laughing) Yes! Sometimes I am in one country and then fly to another country and another country in the same day! Three countries in a few hours. I don't see these places! (Laughing) I don't even know where I am sometimes. I just get on a plane, do the interview then go! Then another plane, then arrive for another interview, then go again on a plane, arrive there for an interview! Let me tell you my schedule, OK?

SP: **OK.**

JC: Now is London, then the day after tomorrow I fly to Paris [12 July 2001] then I'm going to Dublin until the… What's the day today?

SP: **Tuesday the 10th of July.**

JC: 10th… OK, so Dublin until the 25th, then I fly to New York for one day. 26th is the première [of "Rush Hour 2"] in LA… 27th is San Francisco… 28th I fly to Toronto for two days. August the 1st I'm going back to Dublin to start the new movie until… Every weekend in Dublin I have to fly to Toronto for one day for a meeting

with the director, and then go back to Dublin. Then September we start shooting "Tuxedo"…

SP: **You are working with Steven Spielberg on "Tuxedo" aren't you?**

JC: Yeah…

SP: **I don't know why you smile so much - your life is crazy Jackie (laughing). My life is crazy just working with you but… (laughing)**

JC: You know what? I just told Dorothy (Secretary/Personal Assistant) today… You know today I tried to go shopping - but people were chasing me… Afterwards, Dorothy asked me, "Do you enjoy your life?" and I said, "No! Not anymore!"

SP: **You always wanted to be a Hollywood star didn't you? And now you are one, if not the biggest movie star on the planet…**

JC: (Long pause) I really enjoy being by myself, walking around and shopping and doing so many things…

SP: **I've seen it myself being with you in a few countries, London, Rotterdam, Hong Kong, Istanbul, Macau… It is scary when you are out and about and people notice you. But tell all the readers what you like doing if you have some free time. You like relaxing in your house and watching movies don't you?**

JC: Yes! Every movie I want to watch I just call the office and they send it to me, and I watch it at home or my own private office. I watch it by myself (laughing). When I go to the theatre, I sneak in after the movie has already started, so I always miss the beginning! (Laughing) But before the movie finishes I have to run away!!

SP: **Do you still sneak into cinemas and watch movies then?**

JC: For my movies - yes! And some other movies like "Pearl Harbor". But when I go in it's like (Jackie demonstrates waving to people in the theatre). Then some children come to me for autographs… It's very difficult you know, the pressure. But I cannot ignore them… Also it is not fair on the theatre and the people who just want to watch a movie, without knowing that I am there too. No matter how famous you are - you have to be courteous to others. So I always try to do that, and smile! Always smile!

SP: **That's why you have so many fans though, and that's why they adore you so much,**

because you don't ignore them and you give them time if it's possible in between your schedule.

JC: Yeah. It's just… I love my fans. But being Jackie is not easy… Why do I work so hard and give myself so much pressure? But I might as well go on being me, because I am not good at anything else!

SP: *I looked on the Internet the other day and noticed that other stars as big as you don't have an International Fan Club or an all-official magazine or anything… You do genuinely care about your fans don't you?*

JC: Yes, because the fans give me a lot of advice. "We like this!" "No! We don't like this!" So this is why I know how important it is to have this (Jackie holds up a copy of Screen Power), and a Fan Club, and my website. This is why I know when I am going wrong, or I am doing good… I read the letters and everything… Suddenly you see in the magazine: "Oh! I like this movie!" "Oh! I like "Gorgeous"!" "I don't like "Gorgeous"!"… Some like "Crime Story" and some don't. So if all my fans tell me, "We don't like "Crime Story"," then I know I made the wrong decision, and I will never make this kind of movie again. If it's like a 50/50 then I will still make that kind of movie, but try and make it better. So maybe we have "Crime Story 2" and "Crime Story 3". I know with "Crime Story" many people didn't like it because it's too

serious. But definitely everybody liked "Drunken Master 2"… So I need to know what my fans like and what films they want to see. So this is why I have the magazine (Screen Power), my Fan Club and the website for Star East.

SP: *You mentioned "Crime Story" just now. Teddy Chen, who I met and interviewed in Istanbul last year, wrote the script for "Crime Story", and then went on to direct "The Accidental Spy". Were you happy with "The Accidental Spy" and its box-office take in Asia?*

JC: (Short pause) Yeah. It was OK (shrugs his shoulders).

SP: *What would you change if you made "Spy" again?*

JC: Very difficult to say… Sometimes when I hire a director, of course I can totally control it. You can tell at the end that the whole finished movie is 'Jackie Chan Style'. But in the beginning… So this is why in these last couple of years you can see I'm always finding different directors. Right now I'm working with Sammo Hung. I already know Sammo. If I hire Stanley Tong - good! I already know him. So this is why when I hire some director I never knew before… Like I hired you! I don't know what you can do for me. So, OK, I just let you do whatever you do, but I am watching! One, two, three, four – OK! Five - wrong! Then I have to get involved. "Do this! And do that!" It happens on every movie. Like "Crime Story". The director - gone! "Drunken Master 2"? You know the story?

SP: *Lau Chia-liang? Your styles were too different.*

JC: Lau Chia-liang was fired! (Laughing) Yes!

SP: *You were nice though, and left his name on the movie as 'Director'. But everyone knows it's a Jackie Chan movie…*

JC: Yes! But it always happens. Even with Stanley

and I want to shoot for a year!" Now, it's different. Now, we shoot for three months or four months.

SP: *"Highbinders" is for EMG (Emperor Multimedia Group). This is going to be a very quick shoot isn't it? Have you shot the Hong Kong segment yet?*

JC: Not yet. So this is why we're using Sammo to help, and Gordon Chan.

SP: *Gordon Chan who directed "Thunderbolt"?*

JC: Yeah, "Thunderbolt"… I don't like "Thunderbolt" though. As well as myself for

So, we have four weeks to shoot in Dublin for "Highbinders", then I must start "Tuxedo" with Spielberg in Toronto.

Tong. I say, "No! You have to do this! You have to do this shot!"

SP: *So who is your favourite director from the Hong Kong Jackie Chan movies? Who knows your style the best?*

JC: Right now? (Long pause) Sammo Hung.

SP: *Are you looking forward to teaming up with Sammo for "Highbinders"? A lot of people are very excited about you two working together again for the first time since "Mr. Nice Guy" in 1996.*

JC: Yeah. Actually, "Mr. Nice Guy" is not really Sammo's movie. Why? Because he was really controlled by the producer, the budget, everything. Sammo is better now because he will compromise. A lot of people want to hire Sammo now. So now they are saying, "Sammo, Look! With this kind of budget, you have to finish this Jackie Chan film by this date otherwise we lose Jackie! We only have Jackie for two months!" You see? So, Sammo, this time around cannot be like before all those years ago, back in the 80s working for Golden Harvest on films like "Wheels on Meals", "My Lucky Stars" and "Dragons Forever". We could all say to Golden Harvest, "I want this much more money for the budget, and I want this,

this new movie, we're also using a lot of other good Chinese filmmaking people too. But for "Highbinders" they know that the new movie coming up with Spielberg ("Tuxedo") is more important. But for an Asian movie company like EMG - they are a good friend of mine. So, we have four weeks to shoot in Dublin for "Highbinders", then I must start "Tuxedo" with Spielberg in Toronto. But I told EMG, "Don't worry about having to stop the filming of "Highbinders". After I finish "Tuxedo", I am coming back to finish "Highbinders"." Why? Because EMG is a good friend of mine. Friends are so important. So I will finish "Highbinders" and then move onto "Shanghai Noon 2" shooting here in England… I will need advice on how to live here in England for three months for "Shanghai Noon 2"! You will be on the set of "Shanghai Noon 2" right?

SP: *Yep.*

JC: But Dublin first, right? (Laughing).

SP: *Absolutely! What about Media Asia? What's happening there?*

JC: We just did a collaboration with a Japanese company. With Media Asia we changed the group inside. We changed some of the people. But everything is better there now, and we

©2001 EMPEROR MULTIMEDIA (INTERNATIONAL) LIMITED. ALL RIGHTS RESERVED.

very proud and happy to know that when I make a Jackie Chan Hollywood movie there is no "F" word... You know?

SP: *Yes! That's great! Because you have a lot of young fans...*

JC: Yeah... No "F" words in my movies... Just think of how many movies Disney release, like "Mulan"? They cannot put the "F" word in those cartoon movies, because the audience is young and old, like my audience. So my movies are like Disney movies! If you're making a Jackie Chan film - please follow my rules: no sex, no violence with blood, no dirty words and that kind of thing. Always Jackie Chan style! That's what I am most proud of...

SP: *(Laughing) The best style!*

JC: (Laughing) Yes!

> # Now I've succeeded. Now it's like Hollywood call me, it's not me calling them!

shall work on some new projects this year.

SP: *"Gen-X Cops", "Purple Storm", "Gen-Y Cops" were all massive hits across Asia and are finding success in the West too now.*

JC: Yeah, right now I am thinking that I might make a movie with Media Asia next year. We are finding a script right now. (Pause) I'm working on two very interesting scripts right now.

SP: *Secret scripts?*

JC: Yeah...

SP: *Too secret for me to know and to write about? (Laughing)*

JC: Yes! Too secret even for you (laughing)... I will tell you soon OK? (Pause) But, you know me... Jackie Chan style is always interesting... comedy, action and these kind of things. But one thing I am proud of myself is that I tried all those years to get the American market... I tried for so long, and now I've succeeded. Now it's like Hollywood call me, it's not me calling them! And I am

SP: *Jackie, what is your message to all the Screen Power readers around the world who will be reading this interview?*

JC: I love you all! Thank you for all your support. I hope you keep supporting me and enjoy all my new movies... There's still a lot of Jackie to come! So don't worry...

SP: *They will all be happy to hear that...*

JC: Yeah! OK, so I see you in Dublin soon, right?

SP: *Yep! See you soon...*

Thanks to Jennifer Glassman, Linda Russell and Dorothy Wong for arranging our appointment with Jackie, and special thanks to Jackie for giving us a lot of his valuable time from his incredibly busy schedule.

100% JACKIE CHAN
100% OFFICIAL

It's Official, it's endorsed by International Action Martial Arts Legend Jackie Chan and it's here for you to read NOW!!!

"Screen Power" is packed with exclusive interviews with Jackie, his directors, past and present movie co-stars, stunt men, bodyguards and staff, on-set reports from Hong Kong and Hollywood movie projects, reviews, detailed articles, past and present projects profiled, worldwide readers 'Letters Page', competitions (with top prizes!), worldwide 'fans & pen-pal service', and all the latest news and happenings in the Jackie Chan world!

SUBSCRIPTION RATES
(For 4 issues - mail order including all postage and packing)

#1 UK: £25.00
#2 Europe: € 50.00
#3 Rest of World: £30.00
#4 USA: US$45.00

Cheques/Postal Orders in English Pounds Sterling and made payable to "Screen Power". Please allow 4-6 weeks for delivery outside of the UK.

Feel free to email us at: **office@screen-power.com** if you require any assistance or have any questions about subscribing.

GUARANTEE YOUR COPIES
ALL YEAR ROUND
SUBSCRIBE NOW!

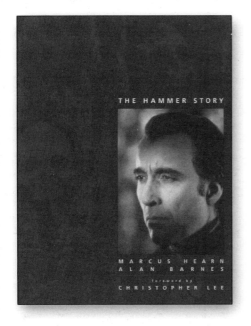